ECCENTRICS, VILLAINS, HAUNTINGS & HEROES

TALES FROM FOUR SHIRES:

Northamptonshire, Bedfordshire, Buckinghamshire & Hertfordshire

by
John Houghton

ALL ROYALTIES TO
ST. MARTIN'S CHURCH,
FENNY STRATFORD

First published May 1994
by
The Book Castle
12 Church Street
Dunstable
Bedfordshire LU5 4RU

ISBN 1 871199 37 9

Front cover: Four shires photo-montage by Norman Kent

Computer typeset by Keyword, Aldbury, Hertfordshire.
Printed at Alden Press Limited, Oxford and Northampton,
Great Britain.

CONTENTS

Preface / About the Author / Bibliography iv

List of Illustrations vi

1. They Made the News 1

2. Ecclesiastical Goings-On 12

3. Shires and Hundreds 21

4. Take Fenny Stratford for Instance 27

5. Hauntings ! 38

6. The Odd Couple of Olney 44

7. Tall Tales 54

8. Crisis and Commotion 62

9. The Mad Monks of Medmenham 69

10. Gunpowder Treason and Plot 73

11. Alban, England's First Martyr 79

12. How Very Odd ! 84

13. A Fence Taken 90

14. Affairs of the Heart 94

15. Not Many People Know That ! 97

16. Highways and Byways 102

17. Fire and Plague 109

18. Sermons in Stones 114

19. Incomers 120

20. The First Shall Be Last 123

Index 131

PREFACE

More than geography links the four shires of Northants., Bucks., Beds., and Herts. For over a thousand years they have shared periods of danger and moments of crisis.

They seem uncertain, sometimes, whether they are the western borders of East Anglia, or the eastern edge of the Midlands! In TV terms, do they 'Look East' or turn to 'Central'?

Perhaps 'Mid-Anglia' describes them as well as anything. And that would be apt, for they have certainly played their part in England's story.

Here, then, are true tales from all four shires. They cover one thousand years and a rich variety of human experience, ranging from the hilarious to the incredible, from the shocking to the uplifting.

John Houghton

ABOUT THE AUTHOR

John Houghton was born in 1916. After graduating at Durham University he was ordained in 1939. He was Curate at Wolverton 1939–1942. He served in Northern Rhodesia/Zambia from 1942 to 1973 and was awarded the Zambian Order of Distinguished Service in 1966. He is a Canon Emeritus of Lusaka Cathedral. From 1974 to 1983 he was National Promotions Secretary in Britain for Feed The Minds. He retired in 1983 and lives in Bletchley.

Also by John Houghton:
Borrowed Time Extended · Tales from Milton Keynes
Murders & Mysteries, People & Plots

BIBLIOGRAPHY

Wm. Bradbrook:	History of Fenny Stratford
Dyer & Dony:	The Story of Luton
Uttley:	Buckinghamshire
Markham:	History of Milton Keynes and District (2 vols)
Wm. Andrews:	Bygone Northamptonshire
Lipscomb:	History & Antiquities of Buckinghamshire
D McCormick:	The Hell-Fire Club
E S Roscoe:	Buckinghamshire
Antony Coxe:	Haunted Britain
Michael Wood:	Domesday
AA:	Secret Britain

PHOTOGRAPHS:
The Cover Picture and other photographs with the initials NK are by Norman Kent.
Photographs with the initials JH are by the author.

WATLING STREET MAP

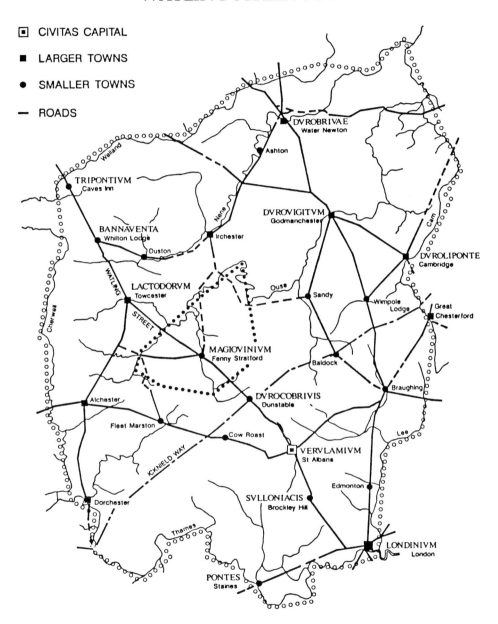

- ▣ CIVITAS CAPITAL
- ■ LARGER TOWNS
- ● SMALLER TOWNS
- — ROADS

The Watling Street crosses our four shires and its staging posts grew into towns.

LIST OF ILLUSTRATIONS

Page

John Hampden & Ship Tax 6
Hampden's Statue, Aylesbury 7
John Howard's Statue, Bedford 8
Castle Ashby 9
Thornborough Church 13
William Dodd 17
Wing Church 17
Water Stratford Church 19
Mediaeval Sheriff 21
Jesse James Poster 22
Dorchester Abbey 26
Magiovinium plan 29
Chantry House, Fenny Stratford 32
St. Martin's, Fenny Stratford 34
Lace-maker at work 36
Passenham Church pulpit 40
Passenham murals & stalls 40
John Newton 45
William Cowper 49
Orchard Side House, Olney 52
Brixworth Church 55
Hanslope Spire 57
Olney Bridge & Spire 57
Buckingham Parish Church 57
Drayton Parslow Church 59
Bell ropes, Nether Winchendon 60
West Wycombe Church 71
Gayhurst Manor 74
Charles I 75
Oliver Cromwell 76
Martyrdom of St. Alban 80
St. Alban's Abbey 81
Soulbury boulder 86
Roman Roads map 104
Dunstable Priory 106
Sundial, Stony Stratford 113
Northampton Fire Plaque 113
Triangular Lodge 115
Tickford Bridge 125
Bletchley Park 128
Bletchley Park map 129

Chapter 1

They Made the News

Eccentrics one and all

Some eccentrics were villains – others were heroes. Our four shires provide examples of all of these. Of eccentrics, there was Henry Trigg, a grocer of Stevenage. He requested in his will in 1724 that when he died his coffin should not be buried in the churchyard, but laid on the rafters in his barn where all could see it. His wishes were complied with and his coffin on the rafters became a regular tourist attraction. Later, it is true, Grocer Trigg's bones were given a more conventional burial. But his coffin is still there on the rafters in Stevenage. You can see it, if you wish, by applying to the Midland Bank in the High Street.

Then there was 'Drunken Barnaby' who put Wansford on the map in his own way. 'Drunken Barnaby' wrote a Journal in very racy style in the 17th century, describing four journeys he had made. In the course of one of them, as he relates, he fell asleep on a haycock by the River Nene in Northamptonshire. He slept so soundly that he was unaware that the river had risen in flood. The haycock floated down the river with the sleeping 'Drunken Barnaby' still on board. At last he woke up and had no idea where he was. He panicked – perhaps he had been carried in his sleep right across the sea into foreign parts! Seeing some people on the bank he called out: 'Where am I?' 'Wansford', they replied. 'You mean Wansford in England?' asked 'Drunken Barnaby'. Relishing this old tale people still talk about 'Wansford in England'. and the pub there is still called The Haycock.

Sir Pexall Brocas

Was Sir Pexall Brocas an eccentric or a villain? Either way he certainly had a distinctive name. He was Lord of the Manor of Little Brickhill in Buckinghamshire, but preferred living it up in London to living in his manor in the country. He was a notorious ladies' man and was said to have fathered one hundred children. For this scandalous behaviour he was haled in October 1613 before an ecclesiastical court which charged him with 'secret and notorious adulteries with diverse women'. He was ordered to stand for two days, clad in a white penitential gown, on the steps of St. Paul's. Released, and unabashed, Sir Pexall Brocas called for his cronies. Then they, all thirty of them, clad in scarlet, made their way to the Guildhall and loudly demanded dinner from the Lord Mayor of London!

When plans were made for extending Little Brickhill Church it was naturally assumed that the Lord of the Manor would contribute handsomely. But when Sir Pexall was approached he asked if the extended portion of the church would be for his exclusive use. He was told 'No'. In that case, he said, no donation.

When Sir Pexall died, 13th August 1630, he was buried in that church. Or at least part of him was. The rest of him, in accordance with his known wishes, was buried at Ivinghoe Aston where he also owned land. It is not known which half is in which churchyard!

The Lady Highwayman

Another individual who could be classed as either a villain or an eccentric was Lady Catherine Ferrars of Markyate, who was born in 1662. Her house, Markyate Cell, was turned into a manor house when the 12th century Priory of Saint Trinity-in-the-wood was dissolved at the Reformation. George Ferrars bought it and it remained in the Ferrars family. Lady Catherine was the widow of an 18th century Ferrars.

She evidently found her widowed life boring. She took to riding out at night dressed as a man, and played the

Highwayman with considerable effect. Up and down the Watling Street and elsewhere she terrorised many travellers and robbed them. Her very first victim was her own sister-in-law whom she detested. She has been immortalised in two major films. ('The Wicked Lady'.)

It was inevitable that so remarkable a woman would leave behind her many stories. Some of these relate how her ghost can be seen riding wildly across country. She was thought to have amassed a great fortune and many believed that this was hidden somewhere at Markyate Cell. An old rhyme says:

> *'Near the cell there is a well,*
> *Near the well there is a tree,*
> *And 'neath the tree the treasure be'.*

So we come to the villains

Prominent among these is the notorious Judge Jeffreys. None of our four shires would want to claim him as a native son – he was in fact born in 1648 near Wrexham – but Buckinghamshire must admit that he lived for a while within her borders. He bought Bulstrode Park near Gerards Cross and rebuilt the house in 1686.

Nominally he was a Puritan but he sought the favour of King James II who was set on returning England to the Catholic faith. George Jeffreys was knighted in 1677. He became Recorder of London in 1678, Chief Justice of Chester in 1680, and Chief Justice of England in 1683.

In civil cases he was able and judicious. But in criminal cases he proved the willing tool of the Crown. The sentences he handed down became notorious for their severity. He was not called 'Bloody' Jeffreys for nothing. Judging those who had supported the Duke of Monmouth's rebellion, he sentenced many to be hanged or transported, first ordering them to be whipped.

But in the end his assiduous courting of King James II's

favour did him no good, for King James abdicated and was succeeded by William and Mary. The Glorious Revolution of 1688 put Judge Jeffreys in jeopardy. He tried to flee to France, disguised as a sailor, but was caught at Wapping. He was sent to the Tower and there he died.

Stand and Deliver!

There were other villains of a quite different sort – the 'Stand and Deliver!' men, the Highwaymen. The most famous of these was Dick Turpin. His exploits covered wide areas which certainly included Whittlebury Forest and the roads running between Oxford and Peterborough. He was hanged at York.

Almost as well known was Jack Shrimpton who spread terror on the London to Oxford Road, and in South Northamptonshire. He was hanged at Tyburn. Unlike Turpin, Shrimpton was a Buckinghamshire man, born at Penn, the son of a respectable churchwarden!

Then there was 'Jack the Leather', also known as 'Old Leather Breeches'. His days as a Highwayman came to an end when, on the run, he took refuge in some farm stables at Edlesborough. He was dragged out and, after trial, ended his days on the gibbet on Ivinghoe Beacon. Both he, and Dick Turpin himself, figure in ghost stories told in the countryside round Dunstable and Tring.

Captain Slash

'Captain Slash' was not a Highwayman. He was a leader of a gang of ne'er-do-wells whose violent exploits were notorious in the area around Northampton in the 1820s. His name was George Catherall. Occasions like the traditional three-day fair at Boughton drew 'Captain Slash' and his thugs like a magnet. But in 1826 their luck ran out. 'Captain Slash' was arrested and after trial was hanged in Northampton on July 21st 1826. His mother had always predicted that he would come to a bad end and would die with his boots on. Defiant to the end, 'Captain Slash' kicked off his boots just before he ascended the scaffold.

Bishop Burgwash

There is one more villain to consider before we turn to the heroes. This villain, surprisingly, was a bishop. It was said of Henry Burgwash that he was 'neither good for church nor state, sovereign nor subjects'. Other epithets heaped on him were: 'covetous, rebellious, ambitious and injurious'. He was Bishop of Lincoln in the 14th century. Twice he was Lord Treasurer and once Chancellor of England.

How came a man of such eminence to deserve such criticism? The good people of Fingest in Buckinghamshire, at the farthest edge of Bishop Burgwash's huge diocese, could tell you. The bishop owned the Manor of Fingest in the Chilterns. He loved to come there to enjoy the hunting, and to indulge in the good life of the Lord of the Manor.

In 1330, to improve the park surrounding the manor, he enclosed the common lands. The people were incensed, for now they were deprived of arable lands for growing crops and of grazing lands for their cattle. This was no way for their Father-in-God to behave! Hatred for Bishop Burgwash was intense in Fingest, and it did not cease when he died in 1340.

Stories began to be told of ghostly reappearances of the hated bishop, dressed not in episcopal purple, but in a hunting-green tunic. The green-clad apparition, it is said, begged the people to forgive him, and urged them to go to Lincoln to petition his successor to free the enclosed lands, and so undo the harm he had done.

So they took him at his word, went to Lincoln to state their case, and succeeded! The villagers won back their common land. The wrong the villainous Bishop Burgwash had done was now righted.

And so we come to the heroes

Our first hero is very much a Buckinghamshire man, but his fame was country wide.

John Hampden

On 26th June, 1643 Colonel Arthur Goodwin wrote a letter to

his daughter, Lady Wharton of Upper Winchendon:

Deere Jenny,

I am now heere at Hampden in doinge the last duty for the deceased owner of it . . . All his thoughts and endeavours of his life were zealously in for this cause of God's . . . he was a gallant man, an honest man, an able man . . . God now in mercy hath rewarded him . . . I have writt to London for a black suite. I pray let me begg of you a broad blacke ribbon to hang about my standard. . . . I would we could all lay it to hart, that God takes away the best amongst us . . .

John Hampden opposed the levy of ship money.

It was of John Hampden that he wrote this letter. John was Member of Parliament, first for Grampound and subsequently for Wendover. In 1627 he refused to pay his proportion of the general loan which Charles I attempted to raise without Parliament's approval. For this John Hampden was sent to prison.

In 1634 Charles I again tried to raise funds without recourse to Parliament. He did this by extending to inland places the Ship Tax already laid on coastal areas. This infuriated John Hampden who determined to make a stand. His opposition to the king made him a national hero. He subscribed £2,000 to the public service and raised a Regiment of Infantry for the Parliamentary Army. The Civil War followed, with

Buckinghamshire being one of the first counties to join the alliance of those opposed to the king's autocratic behaviour.

John Hampden exhibited personal bravery and generalship at the battles of Edgehill and Reading. On 18th June, 1643 he was wounded in the shoulder at the battle on Chalgrave Field. His death followed, prompting the letter from Colonel Goodwin already quoted. His statue stands in the centre of Aylesbury.

John Hampden's Statue in Aylesbury. (JH)

John Howard, Prison Reformer
Bedford has rightly honoured John Howard with a fine statue. Though not a Bedford man he held high office in Bedfordshire. He had been born in 1726 in Hackney, the son of a wealthy upholsterer.

On his travels in 1756 he was captured by a French privateer and kept as a prisoner of war in Brest. So he personally experienced the trauma of being locked up. When he became High Sheriff of Bedfordshire he was so appalled by conditions in Bedford Gaol that he pressed for legislation to tackle the problem. Two Acts of Parliament in 1774 secured some improvement.

After that he travelled widely and wrote 'The State of Prisons in England' (1777) and 'An Account of the Principal Lazerettos in Europe' (1780).

Bedford's statue of John Howard, Prison Reformer. (JH)

John Howard died in 1790 of typhus contracted while visiting a Russian Military Hospital at Kherson in the Crimea. His work for the betterment of prison life did not cease with his death. The Howard League for Prison Reform, founded in 1866, was named after him. Bedford's statue to him was erected in 1894.

Henry Compton of Castle Ashby

One man's hero can be another man's villain, and vice versa. In 1685 James II became king. He made no secret of the fact that he was a Roman Catholic and wished to see this country restored to the Catholic faith. The Bishop of London at that time was Henry Compton, uncle of the 4th Earl of Northampton at Castle Ashby. Henry Compton had been too young to fight in the Civil War, having been born in 1632. When the monarchy was restored in 1660 under Charles II Robert served in the Royal Horse Guards. But he very soon left the Guards, in 1662, to become a priest.

Twelve years later, in 1674, he became Bishop of Oxford. But within a year he was translated in 1675 to be Bishop of London. He was soon out of favour when James II became king. The king ordered his suspension from office for two years because of his 'Protestantism'. He spent those two years at Castle Ashby.

It was clear that the king's undisguised desire to see Catholicism restored to this country would lead to a crisis. In

Castle Ashby in Northamptonshire. Bishop Compton rescued the future Queen Anne and brought her here.

June 1688 the king accused seven of the Bishops of sedition and had them brought to trial. The plan misfired however, for the seven bishops were acquitted. At this point a number of English Lords ('the Magnificent Seven') travelled to Holland to invite William of Orange to come to England with Mary his wife and to take over the kingdom. Mary had married William in 1677. She was the daughter of King James II, and therefore could succeed to the throne if James II could be ousted. So occurred the 'Glorious Revolution' of 1688. James II abdicated and fled to France where he died in 1701. William of Orange landed unopposed at Torbay and marched on London, where the coronation followed.

Meanwhile, Anne the younger daughter of James II was at St. James Palace. She was in a quandary. While she was opposed to her father's attempts to 'romanise' the country she feared to displease him. Her dilemma was resolved by Bishop Henry Compton who had been deeply involved in the plans to get James II out. Bishop Compton staged a dramatic rescue of Princess Anne from the Palace and carried her off in cloak and dagger fashion to Castle Ashby. Thus was Anne saved, to become herself Queen in 1702, after William and Mary had died.

Francis Atterbury

We have one other person to look at who was thought by some to be heroic, and he too was a bishop. Francis Atterbury was born in the Vicarage in the village of Milton Keynes in 1663. His father was the Vicar, and his son followed his father into the priesthood.

His rise to high office in the church was swift. He became in turn Dean of Carlisle (1704), Dean of Christ Church (1712), and Bishop of Rochester (1713).

But he was unhappy with the Hanoverian succession which had replaced the Stuarts on the English throne. His sympathies were with the Jacobites who wished to see the descendents of James II restored. The risings of 1715 and 1745 were the unsuccessful attempts to bring this about.

In 1715 George I demanded that bishops should sign a declaration of fidelity. Bishop Atterbury was one of those who refused. In 1722 he was committed to the Tower for his suspected support of the Stuart Pretenders. A Bill of Pains and Penalties was passed and Francis Atterbury was deprived of all his offices and was banished from the kingdom 'for ever'. So in 1723 he left England and settled in Paris. He died there in 1732. But perhaps after all he had the last word – his body was brought back to this country and laid in an unmarked grave in Westminster Abbey.

Chapter 2

Ecclesiastical Goings-On

In the past 1,000 years many thousands of parsons have lived and worked in our four shires. The names of many of them are known to us, as the lists on the walls of many a church testify. They include many who were scholarly, holy, active, compassionate. And, inevitably, there will have been some, a minority, who were the reverse. If in this chapter we collect together some in the second category it is with the understanding that we are dealing with a tiny minority.

Until the Reformation, in addition to parish priests, there were also several thousand monks and friars. At the dissolution of the abbeys and priories these were turned out, and many of them carried on as part of the parochial ministry.

There is a story told of a Bishop who listened patiently to a tirade of complaints against the clergy. At the end the Bishop said with a sigh: 'The trouble is that when we ordain anybody we only have the laity to choose from'. He meant, of course, that the clergy share a common humanity with everybody else, with the same foibles and frailties. Not surprising, then, that occasionally there have been eccentrics, charlatans, and even villains who were 'members of the cloth'.

Bogus!
In about 1660 the Reverend Joseph Newell arrived in the parish of Thornborough in Buckinghamshire to become its rector. His ministry there lasted thirty years. There was only one snag. He was bogus! He was not a 'Reverend' and he never had been. Yet for thirty years in Thornborough he administered the

Thornborough Church. For 30 years in the 17th century it had a bogus Rector. (JH)

sacraments, baptising, marrying, celebrating the Holy Communion – in short doing all the things that a parson does, yet he never was a parson! How this could have happened defies imagination. Browne Willis in his 'History of Buckingham' records the matter thus:

> *'Joseph Newell, Anno Domini 1663. This person continued to serve this parish of Thornborough, though never in Orders, as I have been informed, for near thirty years. And though he took out the Bishop's Title, on November 7th 1688, being detected for Want of Orders, was obliged to retire and leave the Parish. He went to Pottersbury and died there I was told.'*

Horoscopes

Thornton is the next door parish to Thornborough. Its Rector was the Reverend William Bredon who began his ministry there in 1616. Unlike Joseph Newell, Bredon was the genuine article, a properly ordained priest. He had one unusual attribute – he was an enthusiast for fortune-telling. Browne

Willis wrote of him:

'We are told that this William Bredon was the most Polite person in this age for calculating Nativities, and that he had an hand in composing Sir Christopher Heydon's "Judicial Astrology". There are still remaining in the Parish several traditional stories of his Conjurations and foretelling of events. He died and was buried here July 16, 1638'.

In other words the Reverend William Bredon was good at horoscopes. He claimed to be able to predict a person's future based on the zodiacal data at the time of birth, and by studying the configuration of the planets at a particular moment. So eat your heart out, Russell Grant. The Reverend William Bredon of Thornton was practising your art 350 years ago.

In calling the Rector 'the most Polite person' Browne Willis was not referring to his manners. He was using the secondary use of the word 'polite', meaning cultivated or skilled.

Tally Ho!

An old book, long out of print, called 'Echoes of old county life' contained this account of a former Vicar of Simpson in North Buckinghamshire:

'Another old occupant of the debtor's prison some time afterwards was an eccentric country parson, the Rector of Simpson. He was of good family, and rejoiced in the name of "Tally Ho! Hanmer", a reckless fox-hunting parson of not much credit to his cloth. I never saw this amiable cleric in any other costume than mahogany-coloured top-boots and a square-cut black riding coat, with black breeches, crowned by a peculiar low black hat with a broad flat brim.

When Tally Ho! Hanmer was in very low water he would borrow a sovereign or a five pound note with garnished tales of great distress from many an old college friend. On one occasion a generous individual, touched by a sad story of his, forked out a five-pound note to enable the lively rector to go home to his Buckinghamshire parish to perform his Sunday duties. The donor told a mutual friend of mine and his of his action, and was astonished to hear that he had been fleeced. They were both going

*to dine at Long's Hotel in Bond Street and on entering the
passage, there, not to be mistaken, hung Parson Hanmer's hat.
They entered the coffee-room, the impecunious rector was there,
supplied with a most recherche dinner and a bottle of champagne
at his elbow, spending the five pounds kindly lent him to go home
to his duties. He brazened the situation out, finished his repast,
wished his friend good-night, and went on to the play.*

*This frolicsome parson owed my father about £190 for food
supplied to him in prison. My father never was paid a farthing of
it.*

*He was popular in his parish for all his faults, charitable to the
poor, and, I have been told, preached excellent sermons. His
rectory house was generally barricaded against creditors
throughout the week, and only on Sundays could he walk about in
its grounds and visit his parishioners.*

*These were men of the past. "Tally Ho! Hanmer" was a
rollicking jolly sportsman, a bachelor, and of a type of a class once
very prevalent in England. For good or ill such men are no more'.*

Perhaps a Stoke Hammond vicar was another such. He
wasn't as colourful a character as Hanmer of Simpson, but he
was something of an eccentric. He lived alone in the rambling
old rectory and was a familiar sight as he made his way home
from the Dolphin Inn carrying his bottle of whiskey in an
oilcloth bag. The main railway line passed in a cutting nearby,
and the parson was convinced that the engine drivers sent him
coded messages on their train whistles.

Eleven Tenths

Tally Ho! Hanmer was not the only parson to go to prison for
debt. So did the Reverend John Gould, Rector of St. Mary and
All Saints, Beaconsfield. In fact he died while still in Newgate
Prison in 1866. He had been rector of his parish for forty-six
years. For much of that time he had a running quarrel with the
local farmers over matters of tithes.

The tithe was one-tenth of the produce of the land given to
the Church at first voluntarily, but made compulsory by the

end of the 8th century. The 'great' tithes were those of major crops, the 'small' tithes those of lesser produce. Over the centuries tithes became an important item in the income of the parson. They were often a source of friction between the clergy and their parishioners, as a popular jingle testified:

'We've cheated the parson, we'll cheat him again
For why should the vicar have one in ten?'

This was certainly the case at Beaconsfield. The farmers there reckoned that if the tithe of their corn was taken after it had been stacked into shocks for drying, they should be credited for the extra labour involved. They computed this as entitling them to having to pay only one in every eleven shocks of corn, not one in every ten. The Rector didn't see it that way of course, and the argument grew fierce. The farmers stuck to their point and erected a Tithing Stone at Holtspur near Beaconsfield recording their victory. The Tithing Stone is still there. It is dated 1827 and its inscription says that the 'custom of tithing corn in this parish is (and has been so immemorially) by the tenth cock and the eleventh shock'. In other words the tithe was one-tenth before the corn dried but only one-eleventh after it had dried.

Hanged at Tyburn

It was a bad old custom in times past for clergy sometimes to be appointed to livings, and to draw the income and tithes from them, while not themselves living and working in the parish. Absentee rectors would install poorly-paid curates to do the work. The iniquity of the system was often compounded by the same man simultaneously holding more than one living. In other words he would not only be an absentee Rector, he would be absentee rector of several parishes held in plurality.

A gross example of this is the Reverend Dr William Dodd who held in plurality no less than three parishes – Wing, Chalgrove and Hockliffe. He lived in none of them, though no doubt he visited each at least often enough to collect his tithes! Meanwhile he lived in London where he had built his own

WILLIAM DODD, LL. D.

The Vicar who was hanged at Tyburn.

chapel to which crowds, including royalty, flocked to hear him preach. As a flamboyant dresser he was nicknamed the 'Macaroni Parson', Macaroni being the 18th century word for a dandy.

Dr Dodd lived way beyond his means and was heavily in debt. In February 1777 he did a desperate but foolish thing. He forged a bond for £8,400 at a stockbroker's, making out that the money was for the Earl of Chesterfield to whose godson he was tutor. The fraud was quickly detected and he was put on trial and found guilty. Such an offence in those days was one of the very many that carried the death

Wing Church, one of three held in plurality by William Dodd. (JH)

17

penalty. So it came about that on June 17th 1777 the Rector of Wing (and Chalgrove and Hockliffe) was publicly hanged at Tyburn. He was forty-eight.

Judgment Day

Fundamentalism, religious mania and mass hysteria were all ingredients in the astonishing happenings in the little village of Water Stratford near Buckingham. The small church there is Norman in origin but in all its long history there had been nothing to match what went on there between 1674 and 1694.

It all started with the vicar's obsession. The Reverend John Mason held a very fundamentalist view of scripture and was obsessed by biblical chronology. He spent years developing his notion that by assigning dates to all the events recorded in the Old Testament he could determine exactly when creation had begun. After years of study he published his conclusions. And they were rejected out of hand. This blow coincided with the death of his wife. Perhaps the two blows coming together were the reason that at this point a religious mania overtook him. While in the past he had looked back to the creation, he now became increasingly obsessed with looking forward to the coming Day of Judgment and the end of the world. Just as once he was certain that he knew the exact date of creation, so now he claimed to know the exact date of the coming Judgment Day. And it was going to be very soon! What is more, the vicar announced that when Judgment Day came, and all the world was destroyed by divine fire and sword, the one and only safe place, the only haven, to be spared, would be the little village of Water Stratford.

News of his Hellfire preaching spread far and wide. The little church could not accommodate all who came to hear. So John Mason preached standing at an open window in the church so that the packed congregation inside, and the greater numbers packed in the churchyard outside could all hear his message.

From this point onwards mass hysteria set in. People in villages some distance away sold their homes and moved into

Water Stratford Church, scene of hell-fire preaching and mass hysteria in the 17th century. (JH)

Water Stratford. Night and day the village was crowded. Frenzied dancing and singing and clapping went on nonstop by day and night.

The Church authorities sent a senior clergyman named Maurice to assess what was going on. He was appalled by what he found. Such hysteria was neither healthy nor safe. At the vicarage he tried to see John Mason but was prevented by the crowds, all dancing like dervishes. John Mason, as it happens, lay upstairs in a vicarage attic, in a sort of coma. Within a month he died.

But his death, far from bringing the hysteria to an end, only momentarily increased it. For John Mason had warned people that though he would die, he would be resurrected after three days. Soon there were those who claimed to have seen him.

A priest named Rushworth was given the unenviable task of succeeding John Mason. He even went to the length of opening up John Mason's grave so that people could see that his body was still there.

Very gradually the drama and the hysteria subsided and normality returned to Water Stratford. But some of those who had come from outside stayed on, still convinced that John Mason had been right and that Water Stratford would be the one safe haven when Judgment Day came. John Mason might have got the date wrong, they reasoned, but his parish was still the place to be when fire and sword destroyed the rest.

The Priest who became a Mad Monk
One of the saddest clerical figures of the 18th century was Charles Churchill. His father had been curate at Rainham. It was an impoverished household where the curate 'pray'd and starved on £40 a year'. To eke out a living he brewed cider and carried on an illicit trade with the villagers. He forced his son Charles also to become a priest, much against his will. But soon after his father died young Charles severed all links with the church.

He was a talented young man with a flair for poetry and for satire. He could be compassionate too, and would go out of his way to help a friend. But it has to be added that he was also a rake. He soon found himself in very strange company and he became one of the 'mad monks of Medmenham' (see Chapter 9).

His dissipation encompassed heavy drinking and brothels, and the goings-on at West Wycombe. In November 1764 he travelled to France to visit John Wilkes in Paris. There was a great drinking session and it proved to be the last for Charles Churchill. He died, worn out by his excesses on November 4th 1764, aged only 32.

Chapter 3

Shires and Hundreds

Think of Wild West films and sooner or later you will think of the Sheriff. He is the man with the badge, the Law and Order man. His office and the title he bears are a direct export from this country to the 'new world', for the American Sheriff is the 'new world' version of the Shire Reeve in old England.

The word shire comes from the Old English word scir, meaning an office or duty. And the word reeve comes from another Old English word gereva, meaning the local representative of the king. Put the two words together, shire and reeve, and you get the Sheriff, the local representative of the ruler, the Law and Order man. And perhaps the Sheriff of

A medieval Sheriff arrests a villain in England.

Nottingham springs to mind – the Law and Order man who tried, usually unsuccessfully, to contain the activities of the outlaw Robin Hood, just as an American Sheriff might have to do battle with a Jesse James.

The Shires are areas of England, of unequal size, which later came to be called Counties. And a County can be defined as an administrative, political, and judicial subdivision of the country.

PROCLAMATION
$5,000⁰⁰
REWARD
FOR EACH of SEVEN ROBBERS of THE TRAIN at WINSTON,MO.,JULY 15,1881, and THE MURDER of CONDUCTER WESTFALL
$ 5,000.00
ADDITIONAL for ARREST or CAPTURE
DEAD OR ALIVE
OF JESSE OR FRANK JAMES
THIS NOTICE TAKES the PLACE of ALL PREVIOUS REWARD NOTICES.
CONTACT SHERIFF, DAVIESS COUNTY, MISSOURI IMMEDIATELY
T. T. CRITTENDEN, GOVERNOR
STATE OF MISSOURI
JULY . 26 . 1881

An American Sheriff hunts a villain.

The division of England into counties or shires was pretty well complete by the 10th century. As a unit of administration, each County had a Court which met twice a year and was presided over by the King's representative, the Shire-reeve, the Sheriff.

The Sheriff was responsible for law and order in his own county. He was also expected to provide food and animals for the King's use when the King visited the county. He also had the duty to recruit soldiers in time of war. The Sheriff and his men acted as a kind of police force at a time when police forces as we now know them lay far in the future. The Sheriff had power to recruit extra men when needed to deal with crime or unrest. He could declare a man an 'outlaw', take possession of his property, and have the outlaw hanged if he was caught and convicted. From about 1250 the County Sheriff was no longer responsible for the control of royal forests, and by about 1400 many of his duties were taken over by Justices of the Peace.

Each county or shire was divided into Hundreds. Each Hundred had its own Court meeting, the Moot, held regularly, perhaps every three or four weeks. The Hundred Moots dealt with both civil and criminal trials. They could handle transfers of property. In broad terms a Hundred comprised a hundred families or households. Again, in broad terms, each Hundred would amount to about 100 hides of land, a hide being about 120 acres.

It is to Alfred the Great (840–901) that we owe this division of England into Counties and Hundreds. Before his time the whole area had been divided into parishes. By grouping parishes into Hundreds, and putting adjoining Hundreds into Shires, Alfred created a pattern whose organisation made for better civil administration. It is against that background that we can view the emergence of our four Shires of Northamptonshire, Buckinghamshire, Bedfordshire and Hertfordshire.

But there is a complication which we must take into account. By the year 876 invasions from Scandinavia had led to Scandinavian settlements covering more than two-thirds of England. Only Wessex, comprising the whole of southern England from Cornwall to Kent remained intact.

Danelaw

The Danes proved the greatest threat. They had conquered Northumbria, Mercia and East Anglia. Only Alfred had been able to stem their advance. If he could not remove their threat altogether, he did at least contain it. He ensured that the Danes were kept to a huge area of their own, the Danelaw. The boundary at which Danish rule and power terminated was of crucial concern to our four shires. That boundary ran along the Watling Street down to Stony Stratford and then along the Ouse to Bedford. The effect of this was that while Buckinghamshire was safely on the Mercian side, large parts of the other three counties were within the Danelaw. Not until the beginning of the 11th century was all England united as one kingdom, free from further incursions from Scandinavia. But by then a new and greater threat loomed – the Norman invasion of 1066.

The Normans

William the Conqueror, as cousin of the English king, Edward the Confessor, laid claim to the English throne, maintaining that it had been promised him by King Edward. Having defeated Harold at the Battle of Hastings he advanced on London. His route to the capital passed through our region – over the Thames at Wallingford, through Buckinghamshire across the Vale of Aylesbury to the Brickhills, and thence along the Watling Street to Berkhamsted where a Peace Treaty was agreed. So the Conqueror came to London and there, on Christmas Day 1066 he was crowned in Westminster Abbey.

Domesday

Twenty years after the Conquest, in 1086, William set about the great survey which we know as Domesday. It was an astonishing achievement. The Commissioners traversed the country to assemble the data which William needed. The Anglo-Saxon Chronicle says:

'so strictly did he have the country investigated that there was no single hide nor a yard of land, nor one ox nor one cow nor one pig that was left out and not put down in his record'.

Incredibly, the whole survey was then written up, all 888 pages of it, in a single year. How thorough the exercise was is shown by the fact that the Commissioners made their rounds not once but twice, so that on the second circuit possible frauds could be checked. They were mandated to ask twenty questions about each manor. Those interrogated were required to answer under oath and held liable to severe penalties if they defaulted or cheated.

The result is a highly condensed catalogue of every manor in every county. So we know, in impressive detail, what was the state of the land which made up Northamptonshire, Buckinghamshire, Bedfordshire and Hertfordshire in that year of 1086.

William had a triple motive for carrying out this colossal survey. The aim was, first, to let the king know precisely what geld or tax he could expect from every part of his kingdom. Second, he needed to know what service he could expect from each landowner. And third there was a legal purpose. In the years following the Conquest there had been violent and unjust seizure of lands on a vast scale. That had to be stopped, and Domesday would show who could or could not hold land. Domesday, then, was a Tax Inquest, a feudal record, and a judicial statement.

How was William able to accomplish so much and so quickly after his conquest? The answer in large part is to be found in that whole pattern of Shires and Hundreds which we have already described. The fact is that William had conquered a country in which trained officials were in charge of central and local government. The Shires and Hundreds system was already so organised that every man had a Lord, and every man was reachable by justice and the tax man. Every village belonged to a Hundred whose Court or Moot met every three or four weeks, and every Hundred belonged to a Shire whose Court met every six months. Such was the highly organised system of administration already in place, ready-made for William I to take over. So the governmental system of late Saxon England became an instrument of expropriation once in foreign hands. It could be used to effect the massive transfer of English lands into Norman hands. So perhaps it could be said that Anglo-Saxon England had been too efficient for its own good!

Within twenty years of the Conquest, out of 180 really large landowners, only two were English. Out of 1,400 lesser tenants-in-chief in pre-Conquest days, only 100 English remained. Of some 6,000 pre-Conquest sub-tenants a fair number survived, but they now leased land they had free° owned before 1066.

By 1080 only one of the sixteen English Bishoprics was held by a native. Six of the sees had moved from their historic centres to bigger towns which were centres of Norman administration. And some former seats of Bishoprics ceased to exist altogether. Dorchester-on-Thames is a case in point. Dorchester had been a bishopric in the Kingdom of Mercia, its jurisdiction extending over the whole of the Midlands and including Lincolnshire. The seat of the bishops remained at Dorchester until the Norman Conquest, but in 1072 Lanfranc signed the charter ordering the See to be moved to Lincoln.

Dorchester Abbey lost its Cathedral status in 1072. (JH)

Chapter 4

Take Fenny Stratford for Instance

Anyone wishing to build up a history of any of the towns in our four shires would need to assemble among the building blocks: The Romans, the Dark Ages, Danish invasions and the Danelaw, The Norman Conquest and Domesday, Manors and landowners, plagues, the Reformation, and the Civil War.

Early this century William Bradbrook, Secretary of the Buckinghamshire Archaeological Society, embarked on just such a task. His subject was his own town of Fenny Stratford. His book, 'The History of Fenny Stratford', was published in 1911. It wasn't a large book. It wasn't a large edition either – in fact only thirty-seven copies were printed. Nowadays you would be fortunate to find a photostated copy in the Reference Section of some of our libraries.

If Bradbrook's little book was potted history, what follows is 'potted Bradbrook', as we 'take Fenny Stratford for instance'. It is the story through the centuries of one small town, but it illustrates how many others of the small towns in our four shires evolved.

Fenny Stratford – 'the marshy or fenny fording-place on the street'. The stream called the Ouzel or the Lovatt followed a sinuous course through low-lying meadows. The road or pathway led to the shallows where it was possible to wade across the river. It was at this point that the great trunk road laid down by the Romans passed through, built in strata of material raised above the level of adjacent land. Where the 'street' could cross by a ford over the Ouzel in a 'fenny' but convenient place, a hamlet came into existence and became in time the Parish and town of Fenny Stratford.

But before then, to the Romans, it was Magiovinium. Probably about 40 or 50 AD the Italian Governor or General chose an eligible building site on elevated ground on the south side of the Ouzel ford and there constructed Magiovinium, roughly midway between Durocobrivis (Dunstable) and Lactodorum (Towcester). Coins have been found there, and traces of a fosse and vallum.

The Romans departed from this country early in the 5th century. A long period of deterioration of law and order then followed, with neglect and even destruction of roads. The 5th and 6th centuries were marked by alien invasions of Teutons, Angles and Saxons.

By the 7th century Fenny Stratford was included in the Kingdom of Mercia. The great military road laid down by the Romans received the name by which it is still known – the Watling Street. Fenny Stratford was uneasily poised on the boundary of the Danelaw, Mercia having succeeded in confining the Danes to the other side of the great road.

In 1066 the Normans came. After defeating Harold, the Normans crossed the Thames and marched through Risborough, Waddeston, Claydon, Buckingham and Wolverton. Their left wing ravaged as far as Hanslope, and their right wing moved through Cublington, Linslade and the Brickhills. Then the whole force marched south, leaving behind a devastated country in its rear and received the final submission of the English leaders at Berkhamstead before entering London.

Domesday Book mentions neither Bletchley nor Fenny Stratford, but does mention 'Etone' – that is, Water Eaton, which is in the Digelai Hundred. Before 1066 Water Eaton was owned by Eadgifu, the wife of Wulfward who enjoyed the favour of Queen Edith who owned the adjacent manor of Seciniestone (Simpson). After the Conquest William the

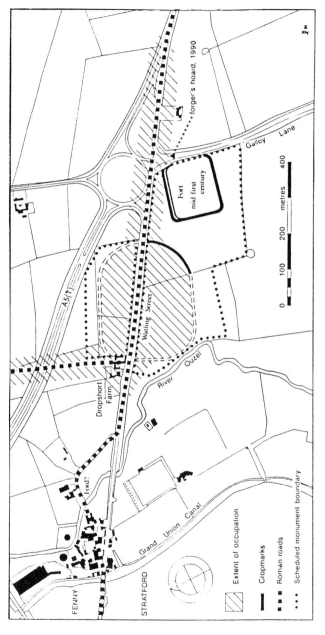

Magiovinium on the Watling Street became Fenny Stratford.

29

Conqueror bestowed Simpson, Water Eaton and other manors covering Bletchley and Fenny Stratford on Geoffrey, Bishop of Coutance. But the Bishop forfeited them all when he supported the claims of Robert to the throne. The manors were granted instead to Roger de Cauz.

In the reign of Henry III (1216–1272) Fenny Stratford passed into the possession of the de Grey family who had a mansion in the meadows now called Saffron Garden, close to the river and not far from the site of Magiovinium.

In 1269 Sir John de Grey, Lord of Etone (Water Eaton) was granted a Charter for a Fair at Fenny Stratford to be held on the eve, day, and six days following of the Feast of the Nativity of the Blessed Virgin Mary.

A later Lord Grey, of Wilton, in 1603 suffered Attainder for trying to oppose the accession of James I to succeed Elizabeth I. The Grey properties were forfeited to the State, and in 1606 the North Buckinghamshire manors, including Fenny Stratford, were bestowed on George Villiers, afterwards Duke of Buckingham.

When James I came to the throne in 1603 the population of Fenny Stratford was about three hundred. In 1607 the King confirmed by Charter a weekly market at Water Eaton, together with a Fair on the 7th, 8th and 9th of April, and another Fair at Michaelmas. But all such markets and Fairs were discontinued during the Civil War.

When that War broke out Fenny Stratford found itself caught in the middle once more. Just as between the 5th and 11th centuries it had been uneasily poised between Mercia and the Danelaw, so again in the Civil War Fenny Stratford found itself between rival garrisons. The Royalists held Oxford and had outposts at Buckingham; the Parliamentarians held Aylesbury and Newport Pagnell. Stony Stratford was held first by one side and then by the other. Fenny Stratford, while not itself the scene of any battle, was painfully aware of fighting not very far away.

The Monarchy was restored in 1660. It was possible then to revive the Market at Fenny Stratford, only to have it discontinued again in 1665 when plague devastated the town.

Epidemics, or pandemic sicknesses occurred at intervals all over the kingdom. Towns and villages on the great trunk roads were especially vulnerable. Fenny Stratford suffered 'plagues' in 1503, 1625, 1643, 1657 and 1658. The visitation called The Great Plague in 1665 was the worst. It was recorded that deaths in Bletchley/Fenny Stratford totalled 106, with a further 23 deaths in nearby Simpson.

In 1674 Thomas Willis purchased the Fenny Stratford Manor. He was a famous physician and neurologist practising in London. His father had been killed in 1643 fighting for the King at the siege of Oxford. Thomas Willis's son later purchased the other manors of Whaddon and Bletchley. When he died his son, Browne Willis, inherited therefore all three manors, Fenny Stratford, Bletchley and Whaddon.

Browne Willis was a minor when he inherited. He came of age in 1702. Given his ancestry and the record of the family in support of the Royalist cause, it comes as no surprise that Browne Willis, who greatly revered his grandfather, was a strong, even bigoted, Churchman and loyalist.

As soon as he came of age in 1702 Browne Willis restored Bletchley Church. He went on later to restore, or help to restore, six other churches, including Bow and Little Brickhill and Buckingham.

In 1705 he was elected MP for Buckingham and held the seat for three years. In 1707 he married Catherine, the daughter of Daniel Elliott of Port Eliot. She brought into the marriage a dowry of £8,000 and bore Browne Willis eight children. She died in 1724 and is buried in Bletchley Church. She was a descendent of Walter Giffard who had held the same manors of Bletchley, Fenny Stratford and Whaddon back in the 11th century.

When Browne Willis became Lord of these manors in 1702 the population of the whole Bletchley Parish was about nine hundred, of whom some three hundred lived in Fenny Stratford and one hundred in Simpson.

Bletchley Parish Church, St. Mary's, had been established in

1155 by the Benedictines. Though there was only the one parish, it comprised three geographically separate entities – Bletchley, Fenny Stratford, and Water Eaton. Of the three, Fenny Stratford was the most important, with its Market and four Fairs a year under Royal Charter.

Though St. Mary's Church in Bletchley was the sole parish church for all three areas, there had been other places of worship in times past. There is a 13th century mention of a Chapel in the house of the Lord of the Manor of Water Eaton. And 15th century records show the existence of the 'Veny Stratford capella', a quite substantial building on the Watling Street in Fenny Stratford. But this had never become a Parish Church, nor did Fenny Stratford become a separate parish. Those developments would come later. Meanwhile St. Mary's Bletchley continued as the sole Parish Church for the three separate areas.

The 'Veny Stratford capella' took on a new importance in 1494 when the Guild of St. Margaret and St. Catherine was founded, based on buildings next to the Chapel, which the Guild used for its worship. The Guild's membership included

Members of the Chantry Guild in Fenny Stratford lived here. (JH)

two priests to minister in Fenny Stratford, 'there being 220 communicants in the said hamlet'.

The Guild lasted just over half a century. Then, in common with all such Guilds everywhere it was abolished in 1547. The Chantry Chapel was abolished at the same time and was pulled down.

The dissolution of the Guild and the destruction of the Chantry Chapel, the upheaval of the Civil War between 1642 and 1649, the successive epidemics and plagues with the consequent loss of trade and travellers, the collapse of Fenny Market – all these factors taken together meant that the little town of Fenny Stratford by the middle of the 17th century was stagnating. At the end of some one hundred years of such adverse experiences, the little town needed something, or someone, to give it new heart and the impetus to develop.

The Restoration of the Monarchy in 1660 brought new hope to Fenny Stratford as to everywhere else. But then had come the Great Plague of 1665 and the Great Fire of London in 1666. The second half of the 17th century saw Fenny Stratford just about hanging on – no growth or development but no great calamities either.

By 1702 the town recovered sufficiently to revive its Market again. In that year too it had a new Lord of the Manor, the young Browne Willis. Could he be the right man at the right time to champion Fenny's revival and development?

Among his earliest initiatives was his purchase of the site of the former Chantry Chapel. He set about raising the money to build a Parish Church for the town on that very site. He petitioned the Bishop of Lincoln for permission to do this. On November 11th 1724 he laid the Foundation Stone of the New church, to be called St. Martin's, and on May 27th 1730 the Bishop of Lincoln came to consecrate it. So Fenny Stratford had its own Parish Church at last. At first it was not always clear just how independent from St. Mary's Bletchley the new St. Martin's Church was. But in time the two parishes were seen to be separate from each other, and each was recognised as the true parish church of its own area.

St. Martin's Church, Fenny Stratford, built on the site of the old Chantry Chapel. Browne Willis built the tower and the north aisle. The rest was added later. (NK)

Browne Willis died peacefully at Whaddon Hall on February 5th 1760 and was buried in St. Martin's Church. He had once said that the building and dedication of that church had been his 'chiefest and most real worldly comfort and happiness'.

Before the Bishop of Lincoln would agree to consecrate the church he had stipulated that some endowment must be provided for the parish. Browne Willis achieved this in three ways: he put up £150 himself; he got £100 from Dr Martin Benson, Rector of St. Mary's; and he obtained an initial £200 (followed later by other grants) from Queen Anne's Bounty.

(Queen Anne's Bounty has a fascinating history. Anne was the last Stuart monarch to ascend the throne. Coincidentally she became Queen at the very time when the young Browne Willis was inheriting his three manors, including Fenny Stratford. In 1704, a year after becoming Queen, Anne set up the Fund which became known as Queen Anne's Bounty, for the relief of the poorer clergy. The Fund was created out of the moneys from the First Fruits or Annates. The Annates, in pre-reformation times had been the payments made to the Pope of a year's income on the appointment of every bishop and other high ecclesiastics. These payments to the Pope had been stopped at the Reformation in 1534, and transferred to the Crown. In 1704 Queen Anne decreed that these moneys should be made over for the relief of the poorer Anglican Clergy. Subsequently the Fund was increased by Parliamentary grants. Finally the Fund was merged with the Ecclesiastical Commission, whose Commissioners today still administer the finances of the Church of England.)

What was happening in the sphere of education throughout this period? It is known that as early as 1587 a schoolteacher was employed in Bletchley. By 1712 William Cole, the diarist/rector of Bletchley recorded that schooling for twenty children was paid for by the Lord of the Manor. Later, Browne Willis at his own expense supplied three Charity Schools at Whaddon. Bletchley and Fenny Stratford. In 1811 the National Society had been founded for the building of National Schools. The Society helped Fenny Stratford to open such a school which was afterwards supported by local clergy and gentry. By 1819 there were 107 children on the register, with an average daily attendance of between 70 and 80. In 1887 all schools were transferred to a School Board.

Fenny Stratford had no settled industry of its own. The cultivation of the soil was its chief preoccupation. In addition, being on the Watling Street, Innkeepers made a living. The Universal Trade Directory of 1792 says the chief manufactuary was white bone lace. Lace-making had already been long established and is mentioned in records from 1638 onwards.

In 1706 the Watling Street was placed by Act of Parliament under the care of Trustees, instead of the Parish authorities. An

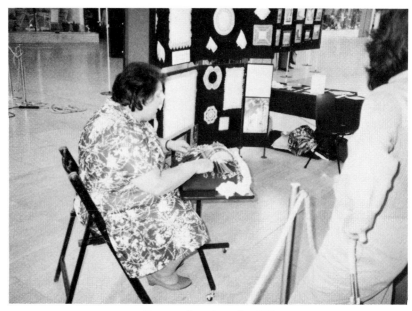

Lace-maker at work. (JH)

Act authorising the construction of the Grand Junction Canal was passed in 1795. The Canal, 147 miles long and with 150 locks, was opened for traffic on July 10th 1801. Two of the locks were at Fenny Stratford, a fillip to the little town.

The London and North Western Railway came in 1838. It had been opposed not only by some landowners, but also by Fenny Stratford inhabitants who didn't want the railway too near to the old coaching road. As a result the main station which should have been at Fenny Stratford, was sited at the extreme edge of the parish and it was named 'Bletchley'. (This prompted a later Vicar of Fenny Stratford, the Reverend J H Firminger, to write: 'So Fenny Stratford had to play second fiddle to Bletchley. The village [Bletchley] had swallowed up the town [Fenny Stratford]. Fenny Stratford's reluctance to have the railway too near to the coaching road was paralleled by Leighton Buzzard's reluctance to allow the new railway to erode usage of the canal. That is why Leighton Buzzard's

Station was built at Linslade.) The Oxford branch of the railway opened in 1851, the Bedford branch opened in 1856 and was extended to Cambridge in 1862.

William Bradbrook's 'History of Fenny Stratford' came out first as newspaper articles early this century, and as a small book in 1911. It obviously therefore has nothing to say about the two World Wars or any of the other momentous events since then. Dr Bradbrook died in 1939. Though the details would vary, much of what he wrote about Fenny Stratford could be matched in the stories of other small towns in our region.

Chapter 5

Hauntings

'A savage place! as holy as enchanted
As e'er beneath a waning moon was haunted
By woman wailing for her demon lover!'

So wrote Samuel Coleridge in his poem 'Kubla Khan'. Notice how in three short lines he gives us a moon, a wailing, and a demon. And in a single line he sets the savage place juxtaposed with the holy and enchanted.

We shall meet all these elements, and many more, in this mini-anthology of hauntings in our four shires.

Phantom Nun
Take Chicksands Priory in Bedfordshire for example. It's ghost story tells of a woman, Rosata, walking in search of her lost lover. She was a nun, and her home, the Priory, could reasonably be supposed to be a holy place, and any nun's lover could reasonably be described as demonic Prosaically, Chicksands is no longer a working Priory and stands today inside an Air Force Camp. In the summer it can be visited one Sunday afternoon a month.

Phantom Bell
At Minsden in Hertfordshire a ruined chapel stands on a hill top. It dates from the 14th century but has been a ruin from the mid-17th century. Yet weddings were celebrated in it up to the beginning of the 19th century. Often it was used for illegal preaching.

In Greek mythology Pan is the god of pastures, flocks and

herds, and Pan it is who is said to appear at Minsden Chapel from time to time. Yet if the god Pan conjures up visions of a sunlit pastoral scene, that is not how it is at Minsden where the dead elms frame a lonely, eerie place. The eeriness is further emphasised by the tolling of a phantom bell. And in 1908, it is said, a spectral monk was actually captured – on film, that is. To complete the saga, in 1949 the ashes of the historian, Reginald Hine, were scattered in Minsden Chapel ruins. He had committed suicide by throwing himself under a train at Hitchin Station.

Still Noisy after Exorcism!

At Abbots Langley in Hertfordshire it is the Vicarage which was haunted, by the ghost of a servant girl. It was said that she had been illtreated by the wife of a former vicar. She haunted not only the Vicarage but also the church. Several of her alleged appearances have been on All Saints Day. Was November 1st, then, the anniversary of some incident in her life time? There are no details of how she died, except that it is said she died a horrible death. In the room where she died the fireplace resists all attempts to keep it in repair. A bishop once exorcised her restless spirit, apparently with some success, except that she is frequently noisy still!

The Black Hound

At Tring in Hertfordshire an old woman was drowned in 1751. It was alleged that she was a witch. The man accused of her murder was hanged in chains near the spot. Subsequently that spot was haunted by a Black Hound. Some said that this animal was the disembodied spirit of a man called Colley. Now Colley had murdered someone called Osborne, and was hanged at the same spot where the murderer of the alleged witch was hanged. So was Osborne the witch? And was Colley her murderer? That would simplify the tale if so.

Northamptonshire gives us one of the odder supernatural tales. It concerns Passenham where no less than four buildings yield their ghostly contributions. From the mill are heard

Sir Robert Banastre ('Wicked Bobby Bannister') gave this splendid Jacobean pulpit to Passenham Church. (JH)

strange noises at night, coming from the wheel. Other buildings which seem to be source or location of mysterious happenings are the tithe barn, the Church, and the Manor House. The occupant of that house in the 17th century was Sir Robert Banastre, Lord of the Manor for forty years. He was a national figure – Comptroller of the Household of King James I, and court Victualler to King Charles II.

To his credit are the very fine murals and elaborately carved chancel furnishing which he commissioned for St. Guthlac's Church in Passenham. Less to his credit are the tales told about his behaviour. He was known as 'wicked Bobby Bannister' and his name was sometimes used to frighten naughty children. 'If you don't behave wicked Bobby Bannister will come and get you'. People claim to have

Murals and chancel stalls in Passenham Church. (JH)

seen him on dark stormy nights, driving madly through the countryside in a coach and pair.

Gooseberry

Of many other odd tales told of Passenham perhaps the most intriguing concerns a lady who was an agnostic. She asked that when she died a gooseberry should be buried with her. If there *is* a God, she explained, a gooseberry bush will spring from my grave. So it was, and it did! So there! At least, that's what they say.

Abthorpe, also in Northamptonshire, boasts two ghosts. One is a Franciscan Friar, date unknown. But the other's date is known. She was Jane Leeson. A tablet on the school wall commemorates her in these words:

'1642. *Feare God, Honour ye King. Jane Leeson hath builded this house for a free school for ever.*'

Some people have said that they have heard the rustling of her silk dress on quiet nights. The date, 1642, with its words: Honour ye King, has a certain poignancy. That was the year when the Civil War broke out, a war that would end seven years later with the defeat and execution of that very king.

Some might wonder whether spirits from the past who appear in places where they formerly lived, are confused by the dramatic changes which have overtaken those places. In Watford there is Cassiobury. It used to be the home of the Earls of Essex. Today it is a Golf Course and a Public Park. On 9th March, 1649, Lord Capel was executed. In the beginning his sympathies had been with the Parliamentarians, but he grew tired of the increasing bigotism of the Roundheads and became a staunch Cavalier. So he ended up on the losing side and was put to death. On the anniversary of his execution, some say, he reappears at Cassiobury.

Likely to be even more puzzled when he returns to the place where he once lived and died is the ghost of a man called Daniel. That place, in Wellingborough, became after his death the Lyric Theatre, and is now a Bingo Hall!

In St. Albans stands Battlefield House in Chequers Street.

People claim to have heard two very contrasting sounds there – the noise of fighting and the chanting of monks. During the Wars of the Roses (1455–1485) a battle was fought near this spot. If the two contrasting sounds are contemporary with each other, were the chanting monks Yorkist or Lancastrian one wonders.

Elsewhere in St. Albans walks the ghost of Mother Haggy. But who, or where or when was she?

Less than five miles away is Salisbury Hall. Charles II bought it for Nell Gwyn. She bore him a child and was angry because the infant had no title. The story goes that she held the child over the waters of the moat and threatened to drop him in. Her royal lover cried out: 'Spare the life of the Duke of St. Albans!'

Nell Gwyn or Nursery Maid?

Winston Churchill's mother later lived in Salisbury Hall. Her second husband was George Cornwallis-West who published his memoirs under the title: 'Victorian Heydays'. In it he recounted how he had once seen a ghost at Salisbury Hall – a young woman dressed in blue. She reminded him of a former nursery maid whom the family had employed. His sister recalled that the family had often remarked on the resemblance the nursery maid bore to portraits of Nell Gwyn. So Cornwallis-West began to wonder whether the ghost he had seen was that of the nursery maid or of Nell Gwyn. To resolve the problem the matter was related in a letter to a well-known medium. The medium replied: 'The apparition you have seen is that of Mistress Eleanor Gwyn who came to warn you of impending danger'. Cornwallis-West ends the recital in his book with the words: 'I knew nothing of impending danger, but within six months a solicitor absconded and let me in for over £10,000'.

Grey ladies, headless phantoms, chanting monks, and ghostly coach and horses – all these are the very stuff of ghost stories. Our four shires have examples of all of them.

Grey ladies appear at Hitchin Priory and at the Great House in Cheshunt.

Headless phantoms appear at Ashwell in St. Mary's Churchyard, at High Down in Pirton, and at Rose Hall in Sarratt.

Chanting Monks we have already met at Battlefield House in St. Albans. They also figure at Amwellbury House near Ware, in Priory Orchard, Kings Langley and at Little Wymondley.

Ghostly coaches and horses are found not only at Passenham, but also at Fulmer in Buckinghamshire, and at Hatfield House in Hertfordshire.

Chapter 6

The Odd Couple

One of the dictionary definitions of Providence expresses the notion that God foresees human needs and contrives to help men meet those needs. We can surely see Providence in that sense in the coming together in one place, Olney, of two remarkable men, Cowper and Newton.

One inevitably brackets them together for the obvious reasons that they were great friends, that they lived for many years in the same place, that they shared a strong evangelical faith, and that they both loved to write. All these are factual dimensions of their association. They exemplify all that they had in common and show the ways in which they resembled each other.

Yet in so many ways they were so different. They truly were an odd couple. They came from such different backgrounds; their separate lives before they met had been so dissimilar.

John Newton – Slave Trader turned Vicar
Anyone who knows anything about John Newton knows that he had been a slave trader and that he later became a priest. The story behind that metamorphosis is truly astonishing. It never ceased to astonish John Newton himself. He himself painted on the wall of an attic in Olney Vicarage (and the words are there to this day) a quotation from Deuteronomy: 'But thou shalt remember that thou wast a bondsman in the land of Egypt and the Lord thy God redeemed thee'.

He was born in 1725, the son of a sea captain. His mother died when he was six and he was packed off to a boarding

John Newton, the former slave-trader, who became vicar of Olney.

school where he suffered both from the brutality of the teachers and from the bullying of older boys. These experiences were curiously paralleled by William Cowper, who also lost his mother when he was only six and was also sent off to boarding school where he was most unhappy. But thereafter their paths were different. Newton left formal schooling when he was only ten, while Cowper continued his education at Westminster School till he was eighteen.

At the age of eleven John Newton went to sea in one of his father's ships. He served on several voyages with neither pleasure nor enthusiasm. Relations with his father were always strained and Newton in his 'teens was obviously an awkward and rebellious character. A friend of his father offered to set young Newton up with a job on a plantation in Jamaica. This would have taken the seventeen year old John Newton abroad for the next five years, a prospect he did not relish.

He paid a visit to friends of his late mother, the Catlett family in Chatham. There he met for the first time Mary, the fourteen year old Catlett daughter and fell instantly in love with her. That further increased his reluctance to go to Jamaica. So, wilfully, he stayed away from home, deliberately delaying his return till he was sure the ship must have sailed without him.

His father, not best pleased, at once arranged for him to join a ship sailing for the Mediterranean. He served as an ordinary seaman and on that one year's voyage, herded in the forecastle with the crude uncouth sailors of those days, he became as crude and uncouth as the company he kept.

As soon as he landed he went to Chatham to visit the Catlett family. Their welcome was as warm as ever, but her parents made it plain that they did not regard a common sailor as a suitable match for Mary.

At this point John Newton's life took a dramatic twist – he was pressganged and found himself an unwilling sailor in the Royal Navy on the warship HMS Harwich. The ship was to sail in convoy to the East Indies, but had to put into Plymouth for repairs. The love-sick John Newton jumped ship in Plymouth, intending to make his way back to Chatham. He was arrested and taken back to his ship in irons. There he was flogged, stripped of his rank as midshipman and made to serve as an ordinary seaman again.

His resentment and self-pity made him a rebel. The Captain of HMS Harwich determined to get rid of him as a nuisance and a trouble-maker. The means to this end were ready at hand. It was the custom in those days that any Navy Captain could rid himself of any troublesome members of his crew simply by swapping them for an equal number of ratings from a merchant ship. So when HMS Harwich reached Madeira Captain Carteret made a deal with the skipper of a merchant ship. He handed over John Newton and another sailor and in return received two ratings from the merchantman.

And that was John Newton's introduction to the slave trade, for the merchantman on which he now found himself was a Slaver. The nineteen year old Newton soon made himself a leader below decks. Soon his morals were as scandalous as any of his new shipmates. He found special delight in blasphemy and in ridiculing all things religious. Towards authority he was obstreperous and unco-operative – all in all a trouble maker.

By chance the ship carried a passenger, a man named Chow. Chow was heavily involved in the slave trade, working from an island base off the coast of Guinea in West Africa. As a way of getting free from his wretched life on the ship, young Newton persuaded Chow to offer him a job. John was later to regret that move. Chow treated him almost as a slave himself, added to which he suffered greatly from fever on that malarial island.

Relief came unexpectedly. Another white trader arrived and set up business on the island and Newton managed to secure employment with him. Then, one day, a trading ship, The Greyhound, put into the island. Newton was astonished to learn from its captain that his father had learned of his whereabouts, and of his plight, and wanted him to take passage on The Greyhound and to return to England. So he sailed home a free man, with renewed hopes that he would see Mary again.

But he was no longer the innocent youth he had been when he first met Mary. Now he was often drunk, always blasphemous, dissolute and depraved. The Greyhound ran into a violent storm in the Atlantic and might well have gone down. The whole crew battled to save her. For eleven hours Newton lashed himself to the wheel and steered the ship through the gale. It seemed impossible that The Greyhound could survive, but she did. She finally drifted into Lough Swilly off the coast of Donegal.

This escape from death greatly affected John Newton. After this there was no more blasphemy, no more mocking at God or religion. He didn't turn saint overnight – his drinking and general debauchery continued, so did the coarseness of his language. But at least blasphemy was a thing of the past.

He was now twenty-five and was offered command of a sailing shop, the Brownlow, another Slave Trader. But he did not feel ready yet for a command and agreed to serve as First Mate. Before sailing he visited Chatham again where he found Mary, now nineteen, as attractive as ever. But there was no talk yet of making her his wife.

The Brownlow was active in the so-called Triangular Trade – carrying trinkets and trade goods to Africa for the purchase of slaves, then ferrying the slaves to the West Indies or America, and then returning from there to England loaded with produce from the plantations.

Newton made at least three voyages on the Brownlow and then, on 12 February 1750 he married Mary Catlett in Rochester. Three months later he sailed again, this time on a ship called The Duke of Argyle, another Slaver. After one voyage on her he was given command of his own ship, yet another Slaver, called The African on which he made two round trips.

By now he was a completely changed man, a reformed character. No doubt his marriage to Mary in part accounted for this, but much more significant was his conviction that he had been saved from illness, hardship and death for a purpose. He was later to express this conviction in perhaps the best known of all his hymns:

> *'Amazing grace! (how sweet the sound!)*
> *That saved a wretch like me!*
> *I once was lost, but now am found,*
> *Was blind, but now I see.*
>
> *'Twas grace that taught my heart to fear,*
> *And grace my fears relieved;*
> *How precious did that grace appear*
> *The hour I first believed!*
>
> *Through many dangers, toils and snares,*
> *I have already come;*
> *'Tis grace has brought me safe thus far,*
> *And grace will lead me home.*
>
> *The earth shall soon dissolve like snow,*
> *The sun forbear to shine;*
> *But God, who called me here below,*
> *Will be for ever mine.'*

But long before he was to write that hymn in Olney there was another crisis to be survived. In 1754 at home with Mary he was preparing to sail yet again – on another ship, The Bee. Suddenly he collapsed and for an hour was insensible. He recovered just as suddenly but the doctor ruled that his sea-going life was over.

He needed then to find a job on shore, and succeeded in doing so. He became a Tide Waiter at Liverpool. A Tide Waiter was a Customs Officer who boarded and inspected incoming ships. For the moment let us leave him there while we take up the story of William Cowper. Neither yet knew, or had even heard of the other. But Providence was about to make their paths converge.

William Cowper

William Cowper was born in 1731 so he was six years younger than Newton. His father was Rector of Berkhamstead and he was born in the Rectory there. His mother was Anne, daughter of Roger Donne, of Ludham Hall in Norfolk.

William's infancy and earliest years were ideally happy. But when he was only six his mother died soon after giving birth to another son, John. She was only thirty-four. William was shattered by his mother's death. Many, many years later he was to express his grief in these words:

William Cowper, poet and friend of John Newton.

> *'My mother! when I learned that thou wast dead,*
> *Say, wast thou conscious of the tears I shed?*
> *Hovered thy spirit o'er thy sorrowing son,*
> *Wretch even then, life's journey just begun?*
> *Perhaps thou gavest me, though unfelt, a kiss;*
> *Perhaps a tear, if souls can weep in bliss –*
> *Ah, that maternal smile! – it answers – Yes.*
> *I heard the bell tolled on thy burial day,*
> *I saw the hearse that bore thee slow away,*
> *And, turning from my nursery window, drew*
> *A long, long sigh, and wept a last adieu.'*

There is a sadly significant phrase in that poem. It is the line in which Cowper describes himself as: 'Wretch even then life's journey just begun'. Remember that he is speaking of himself as he was at the age of six and is implying that even at that tender age he had already started to know depression and melancholy – those parlous states which in later life were to bring him to the depths of despair, and cause him, on at least two occasions, to attempt suicide.

When he left Westminster School at eighteen he began to study law, taking Chambers in the Temple in 1752. He made little or no progress in the profession and was lucky to procure appointment as Clerk of the Journals of the House of Lords. But later he lost that job because he couldn't qualify at the Bar.

In 1756 his father, the Rector of Berkhamstead, died. Young Cowper had to leave the Rectory and the countryside he knew so well. The result of all this was the first of what were to be frequent attacks of depression. In despair he went through the motions of trying to take his own life. He was taken to the Asylum Insanorum of Dr. Cotton at St. Albans for treatment. He recovered in four months but he stayed on there for eighteen months.

He decided to try to find some quiet rural retreat where he could be at peace and write poetry. He chose Huntingdon, partly because it was near Cambridge where his younger brother, John, lived. So he found himself once more living in a Rectory, the Parsonage of the Reverend Morley Unwin. There he became as he said: 'almost like an adopted son'.

The tranquility of that safe haven was rudely shattered when Morley Unwin was thrown from his horse and killed. Always William Cowper found the deaths of those close to him more than he could bear. First his mother, then his father, and now Morley Unwin, almost his second father. Later would come the death of his brother John, and the death of William Unwin, Morley's only son. Much later still would come the death of Mary Unwin, Morley's widow. She meant so much to Cowper. At one time they even contemplated marriage. For many years she was his faithful companion. Each of these deaths had plunged Cowper into despair and depression, and unhinged his mind. Four times he was to know melancholia of the most acute kind.

Now Providence took a hand. Someone suggested to the Vicar of Olney that he should go over to Huntingdon to visit the recently widowed Mary Unwin and to visit the depressed William Cowper. That Vicar of Olney was, of course the Reverend John Newton whom we last left as a Tide Waiter in Liverpool. We need now to resume his story.

In Liverpool John Newton derived increasing comfort from religion. He went to hear all the best evangelical preachers and was much moved by the sermons of Whitfield when that celebrated evangelist visited the city. Newton even began to preach himself, at first to his own household. The notion that he should seek Holy Orders seized hold of him. He was now thirty-three and was determined to be ordained. But would any Bishop take him seriously? It seemed not, and John Newton was nearly diverted in another direction – he was invited by a Presbyterian church in York to become their minister.

Once more Providence took a hand and brought Newton to the attention of Lord Dartmouth. Lord Dartmouth was impressed by Newton and offered him the living of Olney, of which he was Patron. The Bishop of Lincoln agreed to ordain John and so Olney had a new Vicar, the one-time slave trader, now a priest.

It was early in his ministry at Olney that a friend urged him to ride over to Huntingdon to comfort the widowed Mrs Unwin and the melancholic Cowper. Newton urged that they should come to Olney where he undertook to find them a house. So they moved to Olney in 1767. While the house, Orchard Side, was being made ready they stayed at the Vicarage with John and Mary Newton.

Orchard Side was to be the home of William Cowper and Mary Unwin for the next nineteen years. Early during that period Newton was very worried about Cowper's mental health and distressed at his friend's fits of depression. As therapy he urged Cowper to concentrate on his writing. How

Orchard Side House, Olney, the home of William Cowper for 19 years and now his Museum. (JH)

providential it was that in their friendship and in their shared evangelical faith the two men should go on to compile the Olney Hymnbook, the first of its kind ever published in this country. It came out in 1779. It contained 348 hymns of which 280 were Newton's and 60 were Cowper's. Many of them are seldom if ever sung today. But others are classics and continue to be sung regularly. From Newton we have:

> *'How sweet the Name of Jesus sounds'*
> *'Glorious things of Thee are spoken'*
> *'May the grace of God our Saviour'*, and of course
> *'Amazing grace! How sweet the sound'*

To Cowper we owe:

> *'O for a closer walk with God'*
> *'Hark, my soul it is the Lord'*
> *'God moves in a mysterious way'*
> *'Jesus, where'er Thy people meet'*.

In 1780 John Newton left Olney to become Rector of the Parish of St. Mary Woolnoth in London. His departure was a great blow to Cowper. Their friendship continued but their daily companionship was over. Cowper and Mrs Unwin stayed on for a further six years in Orchard Side House. In 1786 they moved to Weston Underwood, living there for nine years. In 1795 they moved finally to Norfolk and there, in 1796, Mary Unwin died. Her death, like all the deaths of those close to him, left Cowper shattered. This time there was no real recovery from his depression. His last years were very sad and his health, both physical and mental, were very poor. He died on 25 April, 1800 and is buried in East Dereham.

There were extraordinary peaks and troughs both in Cowper's life and in his literary output. The same man who gave us the long ballad, 'The Diverting History of John Gilpin', and who so well responded to the national mood in his poem 'The Loss of the Royal George' – a poem that would have come well from a Poet Laureate – that same man could write such sombre words as: *'My fugitive years are all hasting away, and I must ere long lie as lowly as they, with turf on my breast and a stone at my head'.*

The fact is he was so often plunged into deep personal distress, hovering between religious mania and despair, yet at other times could write with delicious humour, wit and charm. We shall never fully know how much we (and Cowper) owe to the influence Newton had on his improbable friend. But certain it is that it was Providence that brought them together.

And it was Providence, too, that brought Newton to London to be of such enormous help to another William, William Wilberforce, in his long struggle to secure the abolition of slavery.

Newton's ministry in London was a long one – he was Rector of St. Mary Woolnoth for twenty-eight years and when he died in 1807, at the age of eighty-two, he was buried there. But in 1893 he and Mary his wife were reinterred at Olney in the churchyard of the Parish where for so many years the improbable friendship of John Newton and William Cowper had flourished.

Chapter 7

Tall Tales

A tall tale is usually a story that is incredible, hard to believe. The stories that follow here are not of that kind. They are tall tales, not because they challenge credulity, but because they are all tales about church towers and steeples, the tallest parts of every church.

What is the difference between a tower and a steeple? All steeples are towers but towers are not steeples. It's the pointed bit on top of a tower that makes it a steeple. The words themselves are interesting. 'Tower' comes from the Latin word 'turris' which also gives us 'turret'. Both towers and turrets are found in castles and forts as well as in churches. So there is nothing intrinsically 'holy' or 'religious' or 'ecclesiastical' about a tower. It does, though, suggest strength and power and in that sense can remind us of such biblical phrases as 'the name of the Lord is a strong tower'. or, as in Psalm 61 'Thou hast been my shelter, a tower for refuge from the enemy'.

Steeples are also called spires. At first sight one might suppose that there is a link here with the word 'inspire'. Inspiration sounds a much more encouraging thought – after all, look how the spire points heavenwards! But that would be a misleading line of thought. Spire has nothing to do with inspire or inspiration, or anything 'churchy' of that sort. Pity, really! If fact, the derivation of the word 'spire' is that it comes from the Old English word 'spir', meaning a blade.

Towers, steeples and spires prompt thoughts of bells, and bells certainly figure in some of the stories that follow.

All Saints Church, Brixworth

Pride of place in our four shires must surely be given to the church at Brixworth in Northamptonshire, and this for several

All Saints, Brixworth. 'The finest 7th century building north of the Alps.'

reasons. First, because of the astonishing age of this church. It was built as long ago as the 7th century, in Saxon times. There are only four completely Saxon churches in the whole country. The other three are St. Martin's Church in Canterbury, Escomb in County Durham, and Bradwell-on-Sea in Essex. All Saints, Brixworth, surpasses them all in its size and completeness. No wonder it has been described as: 'the finest seventh century building north of the alps'.

The second important aspect of Brixworth Church to be noted is that its fabric incorporates a considerable number of Roman tiles. The Romans left this country early in the 5th century. Gradually many of the villas and other buildings they left behind either fell into disrepair or were deliberately pulled down. Building materials from them would not have been wasted – they would have been 'recycled' and incorporated in other buildings. This happened when Brixworth Church was built in the 7th century. The Roman tiles are there to be seen, especially in the arches over windows and in portions of the tower.

Mention of the tower brings us to yet another way in which Brixworth Church is almost unique in this country. Only four churches in England have a stair turret clamped, as it were, on to the outside of the tower. Brixworth Church is one of them. In either the 9th or 10th century the external stair turret was added on the outside of the earlier Saxon tower. Inside it the worn steps of the spiral staircase lead up to the tower chamber.

Two of the finest spires in our region are within a few miles of each other, at Hanslope and at Olney.

Steeplejacks

At 186 feet Hanslope's spire is the tallest in Buckinghamshire. Some time in the 18th century it needed to be repaired. A famous steeplejack, Robert Cadman, was commissioned to carry out the work. He was a extrovert character with two unusual attributes. First, he spurned the use of scaffolding and

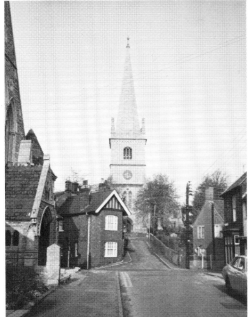

Top left:
Hanslope Spire, the tallest
in Buckinghamshire. (JH)

Top right:
Olney Bridge and Church
spire. (NK)

Buckingham Parish Church
lost TWO spires in 4 years
(1773 & 1776). So they
pulled the church down and
built this one in its place.
(JH)

preferred simply to climb a spire much as a mountaineer might climb a rock face. Secondly, it was his habit to carry up with him a small drum on which he liked to beat a tattoo when he got to the top! On this occasion, true to form, he climbed to the top and beat his tattoo. Only when he finally came down to earth again, after effecting his repairs, did he realise he had left his precious drum on the top of the spire. He was all for going straight up again to retrieve it, but was persuaded to leave it till the next day when he would be more rested. Sadly, he was killed later by falling from another spire elsewhere.

Olney's fine steeple was also the scene of a remarkable steeplejack story. The steeplejack in question was a highly professional expert named Parker. Having carefully erected his scaffolding he decided to rest awhile before tackling the repairs. While he rested a young Olney lad named Charlie came along. He was home on leave from the Navy. Climbing the rigging at sea had given him a great head for heights. He quickly climbed to the top of the spire and from there he entertained the crowd below with his antics. Out came an irate Mr Parker, affronted by such behaviour. Up Mr Parker climbed to teach young Charlie a lesson. Down climbed Charlie, and even when he reached the point in the scaffolding where cunning Mr Parker had removed a length of ladder intending to fox Charlie, all Charlie did was to grab hold of a pulley rope and lower himself to safety, mocking Mr Parker cheekily as he did so.

Buckingham parish church was built in the 13th century. It had a square tower which was topped by a wooden spire clad in lead. It rose to a height of 163 feet.

Disaster struck on 7th February 1698. The lofty spire fell down doing much damage also to the tower itself. Efforts were made to find the money to rebuild the spire. Browne Willis, the Antiquarian Lord of the Manors of Bletchley and Water Eaton, who had once been MP for Buckingham, worked especially hard to raise the money needed. By 1773 the tower was repaired and topped with a new spire tapering up twenty-four feet above the tower. Alas, just three years later, on 26th March 1776, the spire fell again. Soon after this the whole church was demolished and rebuilt on a new site nearby.

Drayton Parslow is not a large village. It is about five miles from Bletchley. Today no trace whatever remains of the bell foundry which once, surprisingly, flourished there. It belonged to the Chandler family whose members formed a sort of dynasty of bell founders. In the 17th and 18th centuries many a bell was cast in the foundry at Drayton Parslow. Succeeding generations of Chandlers carried on the skilful work. The products of the Drayton Foundry hang still in many a tower or steeple, not only in Buckinghamshire but in surrounding counties as well. The last of the Chandler dynasty died in 1726 and there were no more sons to carry on the tradition. But the bells they produced will continue to ring out for a long time to come.

Drayton Parslow Church. No trace remains of the famous bell foundry in the village. (JH)

Drama in the Bell Tower!

St. Andrew's Church at Great Linford has a peal of five bells. In 1756 they were all recast at St. Neots. Bell-ringing is a centuries-old art and it is good that successive generations keep the art alive. But on one occasion at St. Andrew's, Great Linford, the ringing chamber was the scene of a fatality. One of the ringers, instead of letting the rope run freely through his hand, kept hold of it and was carried aloft. When he fell to the floor he was found to be dead.

But something much more sinister once happened in the tower of Great Linford Church. The bells had been ringing for some time when suddenly it was noted that blood was dripping down one of the ropes! The ringing was stopped and the belfry was entered to discover the cause. There, among the bells, was found the body of a man. The account of this tragedy, written in 1900, gives no details as to who the man was or how he came to be in the belfry.

Bell ropes at Nether Winchendon. Similar ropes in Great Linford twice led to tragedy. (JH)

Tornado in Buckinghamshire

'In Herefordshire, Hertfordshire and Hampshire hurricanes hardly ever happen'. That, or something like it, was one of the tongue-twisters Professor Higgins taught Eliza Doolittle to say to improve

her diction. In Buckinghamshire one hurricane *did* happen. The Bucks Advertiser on 26th May 1950 carried this story:

SCAR TWENTY YARDS WIDE ACROSS THE FACE
OF BUCKINGHAMSHIRE
A Tornado ripped its stormy path on Sunday after noon and now there is a trail of damage through Wendover, Halton Camp, Aston Clinton, and out through Linslade to Bedfordshire.

It took the roof off the Baptist Chapel in Wendover. At Linslade 300 houses and several shops were damaged as was the Parish Church tower but it was here that the tornado really spent its fury for it disappeared over the Bedfordshire border and petered out'.

And finally . . .

So far all these tall tales have only been tall because they concerned the tallest parts of churches, namely towers and spires. They have not been 'tall' because they were incredible or defied belief. But we can conclude with one more 'tall tale' which *does* come in the incredibility bracket.

It concerns the 14th century church of St. Mary the Virgin at Marston Moretaine in Bedfordshire. It has a separate tower which originally was a Saxon defence tower. Folk lore says that centuries ago the Church had an argument with Satan, who flung it away in anger. So that is why it is separate from the church!

Another tale relates how one day the Devil took three leaps off the tower. From his first leap he landed in a field one hundred feet away. His second leap landed him on a spot where there was a Pub called The Jumps. (Unfortunately the Pub was demolished in 1930.)

But the third and last leap was the worst. It carried the Devil over the road and into a field where three boys were playing leapfrog. The Devil invited them to jump with him and they disappeared down a hole in the ground and were never seen again! An ancient stone, the Devil's Stone, stands on the spot.

Chapter 8

Crisis and Commotion

In 1380 the English Parliament sat in Northampton. It was not the first time it had done so, but it proved to be the last. It could not sit in the Castle for that was in a bad state of repair. It sat instead in the Great Hall of St. Andrew's Priory.

Poll Tax

That Parliament took what later proved to have been a very unwise decision. It decided to impose a Poll Tax on the entire nation. Every person over the age of fifteen would have to pay one shilling, whether male or female.

The monarch at that time was the boy King, Richard II. His advisers impressed on him that more money was urgently needed to pay for the ongoing war against the French. That war was part of the never-ending Hundred Years War.

To appreciate the blow that this new tax represented to the majority of the population one has to recall that the preceding thirty years had seen the Black Death devastate Europe. It had started on the continent in 1347. Within two years it had carried off a third of the entire population of this country. (See Chapter 17.) The Northampton Parliament was therefore proposing a swingeing new tax which would fall on every individual of a hugely depopulated nation. It was the last straw, and the reaction was immediate and intense.

The Peasants' Revolt

The Government Tax Commissioners were urged to scour the country to identify all those who were liable for the new shilling-a-head tax. Everywhere they met with evasion and angry refusal. Families hid their young teenage sons and daughters. In our four shires, as elsewhere in the country, tax collectors and peasants came to blows. By mid-1381 the protests had become a thorough-going rebellion.

The leader in this Peasants' Revolt was the dynamic Wat Tyler. He came from Essex, but it was in Kent that he was chosen as leader and spokesman, after the peasants had taken Rochester Castle. With Wat Tyler at their head the peasants moved on to Canterbury, then to Blackheath, and finally to London.

In a remarkably short time the peasants had organised themselves into a force numbering nearly 100,000. The King felt obliged to agree to meet with them at Smithfield. But by then many had lost their lives. The Archbishop of Canterbury, and the King's Royal Treasurer, were both murdered.

In an attempt to defuse the situation the young King Richard II promised the peasants that he would establish their rights by a Charter. But as the crowds began to disperse at Smithfield they were attacked by Knights and many were killed. In the confusion William Walworth, Lord Mayor of London, wounded Wat Tyler who was taken to St. Bartholomew's Hospital. Hearing of this the Lord Mayor ordered his seizure and had him beheaded.

Thereafter the Peasants' Revolt petered out throughout the south of England. But it lingered on in East Anglia. Peasant forces from north-east Northamptonshire were still active, laying siege to Peterborough Abbey. There they were attacked and overwhelmed by men-at-arms of the Bishop of Norwich. Many were killed in the Abbey itself at Peterborough. Altogether, in eastern England alone, some 1,500 lost their lives, including many from our four shires.

In considering crisis and commotion in the history of our four shires we relate elsewhere such great national events as the

Gunpowder Plot and the Civil War. (See Chapter 10.) We are concerned here with commotions on a more local scale. And the next to concern us came in June 1607.

The Levellers

Squire Tresham at Newton, near Kettering, had enclosed the open-field arable lands on his estates – to the great wrath of the country folk. Their reaction was dramatic and it owed much to the ardour of a man named John Reynolds. 'Cometh the hour, cometh the man'.

John Reynolds was a charismatic figure. He was nicknamed 'Captain Pouch', from the great leather pouch which he always wore at his side. 'Captain Pouch' put himself at the head of a thousand armed men who called themselves 'The Levellers' – an apt name because they set to work to tear up every hedge they could find.

Landowners and Government figures were alarmed at this turn of events. The Justices of the Peace called for the arming of tenants, and a pitched battle ensued between Levellers and Tenants. The Levellers were ousted and fled, but not before some of their number were killed and others arrested.

The arrested Levellers were quickly put on trial. Those found guilty were hanged and quartered, the 'quarters' being hung up at Northampton, Oundle, Thrapston and elsewhere, *'pour encourager les autres'*. It was something of an anti-climax that after his death 'Captain' Pouch's pouch was found to contain nothing but a bit of green cheese!

The Machine Breakers

1830 was not a happy year in England. A number of factors combined to produce unrest. There were protests against enclosures; wages were low and unemployment was high; the employment of 'strangers' exacerbated the unrest; and the introduction of new agricultural machinery was opposed because it was held to be keeping men out of work.

The result of all these things was a twelvemonth of riots all over the country. Our four shires did not escape. When the riots were eventually brought under control nearly two thousand rioters were in gaol awaiting trial. Of all the prisoners tried, 800 were acquitted or bound over; 644 were sent to prison in this country; 505 were sentenced to transportation, of whom 481 were sent to Australia. And 19 were hanged.

The troubles had started in August 1830, when a series of arson attacks and the destruction of agricultural machines began in Kent. It spread rapidly to other counties, notably Buckinghamshire.

The pattern of events was dramatic. First of all threatening letters were sent, signed by a mythical 'Captain Swing'. The threats they contained were soon implemented. Stacks and barns were set alight, threshing machines were destroyed, and riotous assemblies became the order of the day. Bands of rioters moved from one village to another. Farmers, landowners, and Government itself became alarmed. The Yeomanry were mobilised. Special Constables were sworn in, and many landowners organised their own vigilante-type patrols.

In Buckinghamshire the disturbances followed a pattern somewhat different from those in other counties. There was rather less arson, and less blatant demands for money. Nevertheless many farms were attacked and many agricultural machines smashed. But in Buckinghamshire there was an additional target – the paper mills in the High Wycombe area. These mills had recently installed new machines – for example, one machine was a cylinder with knives for grinding rags, a job formerly done by hand. So the paper makers felt themselves threatened by the new machines, just as did the farmworkers on the land.

In Buckinghamshire as elsewhere the first intimation of trouble to come took the form of threatening letters signed by the mythical 'Captain Swing'. One such letter sent to a Wycombe farmer read:

'This is to acquaint you that if your threshing machines are
not destroyed by you directly we shall commence our
labours. Signed on behalf of the whole SWING'.

Fires broke out on farms at Nash, Wavendon, Marlow and

Slough. The farmer at Slough had received this letter:

'I, Swing, do hereby certify that Mr Way of Denham will before three Knights are over, see a bonfire. Let Mr Lucas of Maidenhead know immediately, or he will see one – also Mr Clarke.
Signed SWING'.

In the face of this rising tide of unrest the High Sheriff of Buckinghamshire called on the inhabitants to hold themselves in readiness to assist him in quelling any disorders that might break out. Night Patrols were organised and the Bucks. Yeomanry was called out. Troops from Olney, Newport Pagnell and Stony Stratford were deployed to Aylesbury and then moved on to join up with other forces at Amersham.

Riots broke out at Stowe where the mob destroyed a winnowing machine, a chaffcutter, and a haymaking machine. At Wycombe the Magistrates called a meeting which began in the Guildhall. On the platform were leading notables, including Lord Carrington. But the meeting had to be abandoned when a mob entered the hall, ejected the Chairman, broke up chairs and tables, and smashed windows.

The mob then went on to the nearby paper mill to demonstrate there. Meanwhile men from Waddeston and Upper Winchendon went from farm to farm smashing farm machinery as they went. Trouble broke out at Stowe again, and at Bishopstone.

By November 1830 many arrests had been made and trials began in Aylesbury Court. But this fact did little to halt further disorder. Mobs attacked paper mills at Bassetbury, Marsh Green and Loudwater. And further attacks occurred on farm machinery at Long Crendon. Forty Grenadier Guards were sent from Windsor to Wycombe where serious riots had continued. By now the Gaol in Aylesbury was full to overflowing.

In January 1831 trials resumed in Aylesbury Court. One hundred and thirty seven prisoners were tried in one week, while further arrests were being made. All were found guilty of riot but some were acquitted of assault. Twenty-one were convicted on capital charges.

By March 1831 the first of the prisoners sentenced to

transportation were sent to Portsmouth. When the transport ship *Proteus* sailed on 14 April 1831 for Van Diemans Land, twenty-nine of the one hundred and two convicts on board were Buckinghamshire men. So ended Buckinghamshire's share in the unrest all over the country led by the mythical 'Captain Swing'.

Boots for Marching – Marching for Boots

Raunds in Northamptonshire faced a crisis in 1905. There had been plenty of work there during the Boer War, because at Raunds they made boots for the Army. But a slump immediately followed when that war ended and wages were cut. A strike failed to get wages restored and a protest march was planned.

It was organised by James Gribble, an ex-soldier. Under his leadership the men marched from Raunds to the War Office in London. The march was so well organised and carried out that James Gribble was dubbed 'General' Gribble. The demonstration achieved its object. The boot-making trade revived.

So 'General' Gribble in 1905 had better success than 'Captain' Pouch in 1607 and 'Captain' Swing in 1830.

Luton Town Hall Burnt Down

Armistice Day, November 11th, 1918 brought the fighting in World War I to an end. But it was June 28th, 1919 before the Peace Treaty was completed. Everywhere celebrations were planned to mark the occasion. Luton Town Council announced that there would be civic celebrations on July 19th, 1919. There would be floats, five bands, entertainment for 9,000 children, and a banquet for the Mayor and Corporation. But, oddly, there was no provision for mass thanksgiving, or for the participation of the ex-servicemen who had actually fought in the war!

There was widespread protest but the Council declined to alter its plans. So a rival unofficial Celebration Committee was formed. This came up with a plan for two days of celebration, culminating in a Thanksgiving Service and a Parade of serving and ex-servicemen. All this would take place in Wardown Park.

But the Council refused permission for Wardown Park to be used. Under pressure, they said the Moor, or Pope's Meadow might be used. This satisfied no one – they wanted Wardown Park or nothing. Church leaders joined in the controversy, on the side of the protesters.

A crowd marched on the Town Hall to voice its anger. The Town Council was in session; the Town Hall was invaded and the Mayor's speech was drowned out by the shouting and jeering. The Councillors fled, leaving the crowd in possession. Furniture from the banqueting hall was flung from the windows into the street.

Twenty-four hours later the Town Hall was again invaded. This time the unrest was more serious. The Town Hall was ransacked, and a fire started. The hoses of the Fire Brigade were slashed, shops were looted, and a lone pianist, on a stolen piano, led the crowd in singing: 'Keep the home fires burning'!

Troops were brought in and the situation might have become really ugly. But tension was relieved because the troops were singing popular wartime songs. Eventually calm was restored. But by then the Town Hall had been gutted and a number of arrests had been made. At the trials, held at Bedford Assizes, the Judge imposed relatively light sentences. He said that while such behaviour could not be tolerated, there had been some provocation.

So, sadly, on that July day in 1919, commotion had displaced what should have been a day of celebration and thanksgiving.

Chapter 9

The Mad Monks of Medmenham

Hugh de Bolebec founded the Cistercian Abbey at Woburn in the year 1200. An offshoot or cell of the Abbey was later set up at Medmenham on the banks of the Thames about four miles from Henley. So the first Monks of Medmenham were there in the 13th century. By the early 16th century Medmenham Priory was annexed to Bisham Abbey on the other side of the river.

At the Reformation all monasteries and priories, including Medmenham, were closed. The Priory then fell into disrepair after the Monks had been turned out. They had never enjoyed any great reputation for piety and were described by some as 'lawless'.

Some two hundred years later there would be other 'monks' at Medmenham, bogus monks, members of the Hell Fire Club, and *their* reputation would be infinitely more questionable!

Sir Francis Dashwood

Sir Francis Dashwood was born in 1708. When he was sixteen his father died and he inherited a considerable fortune. He also inherited West Wycombe House and spent much effort and money to develop the grounds to the attractive high standards they still maintain today.

Nearby were the ruins of the old Medmenham Abbey, and it occurred to Sir Francis that they might make a splendid setting for a fantastic plan he had in mind. The original Abbey had been home for the monks of long ago. Well then, he would bring monks back to Medmenham!

Sir Francis was an eccentric. After travel in Italy he had

returned to England and, with other wealthy friends who had also travelled in Italy, he founded the Society of the Dilettanti, a dining society exclusively for gentlemen of wealth and position interested in fine arts and all things Italian.

He had entered Parliament in 1741, and in about 1745 he had this eccentric notion – bringing monks once more back to Medmenham! From Francis Duffield he acquired the lease of the old Abbey ruins and he announced the foundation of 'The Brotherhood of Saint Francis of Wycombe', with himself as St. Francis of Wycombe!

So began the brief but startling history of 'the mad monks of Medmenham'. They probably never numbered more than thirteen at any one time but they were all men of rank and position. The membership included Lord Melcombe, the Earl of Sandwich, William Hogarth the artist, Charles Churchill, a poet and former priest, Frederick Prince of Wales, John Wilkes, and Paul Whitehead, the satirist and minor poet, who was treasurer. Together the mad monks of Medmenham were members of The Hell Fire Club.

The ' monks' of the mock order used pseudonyms. They wore white habits, but the 'Prior' sported a red bonnet. For their entertainment mock 'nuns' were brought down from London. Inevitably stories spread of shocking goings-on at Medmenham! The word 'orgy' sprang to many people's lips. And even if the stories were exaggerated, there can be little doubt that they were not without foundation.

The heyday of the Mad Monks of Medmenham lasted from 1745 to 1763. Their founder, Sir Francis Dashwood, had already been an MP since 1741. From 1761 to 1762 he was Chancellor of the Exchequer no less, and thereafter Postmaster General from 1766 to 1781. It might seem surprising then that he, and other notable persons who were members of The Hell Fire Club, should be able to combine high public office with such private behaviour. But the fact is that rakish behaviour was a feature of 18th century social life for many. And it could well be that what went on at Medmenham was never as outrageous as many supposed. The stories grew in the telling.

This was certainly the view of Dr Benjamin Bates of Little Missenden. He was himself a member of The Hell Fire Club and was personal physician to Sir Francis Dashwood. He lived to the ripe old age of ninety-eight, dying in 1828. He maintained to the end that people should not credit all they heard about the Mad Monks of Medmenham.

The Golden Ball

Throughout this period Sir Francis continued to take seriously his duties as a great landowner. The surroundings of West Wycombe House and of the Abbey ruins themselves continued

to be developed and beautified. He rebuilt West Wycombe Church, but here too his eccentricity played a part. He built it at the top of a hill and in its tower he set a great golden ball. This glistens in the sun and gives the church tower a unique feature. Just how unique can be appreciated when one learns that the golden ball is large enough to accommodate six or more people. And it often did so. John Wilkes testifies that he took part in a drinks party inside the golden ball with several members of The Hell Fire Club. 'The best Globe Tavern I ever was in' he boasted.

As a conscientious landowner and employer Francis Dashwood (who succeeded to the title of 15th Baron Le Despencer in 1762) embarked on a great road building scheme which would both benefit the neighbourhood and provide jobs for many. For this he needed huge quantities of roadmaking material. He found this ready to hand in the caves of the steep West

John Wilkes and several other 'Mad Monks of Medmenham' held a drinks party inside the Golden Ball on West Wycombe Church tower.

Wycombe hill, from which his employees extracted all the material they needed.

This exercise considerably extended, widened and deepened the caves which were already there. It then occurred to him that these caves would make a more exciting, and less public, venue for the meetings of The Hell Fire Club. Thereafter such meetings took place in the caves.

The Satanic Baboon

Many are the tales told of those meetings. They figured in a novel, called Chrysal, written in the 1760s by Charles Johnstone. One such tale relates how a baboon was introduced to impersonate Satan. This landed on the shoulder of Lord Sandwich and so terrified him that he fled screaming from the caves.

The Hell Fire Club had a motto – *'Fay ce que vous voudras'*. This is only half of the full original version. 'Do as you like' was the Hell Fire Club motto. The full version is: 'Do as you like – *and pay for it!'*

On the whole the Mad Monks of Medmenham and their Hell Fire Club have had a bad press. Perhaps they deserved it. Certainly most references to them in later accounts have been couched in reproving, moralistic language. Thus, Brewer's Dictionary of Phrase and Fable writes of the 'profanities' at Medmenham. E S Roscoe, in his book, Buckinghamshire, published in 1903, writes: 'Their form of amusement was at once profane and childish, mimicking as they did religious rites in their social meetings.' In fairness, Roscoe did add: 'but the character of their gatherings was probably neither better nor worse than that of others before or since'. But then he spoils this seeming fairness and even-handedness by continuing: 'From the positions of those who took part they have achieved a disagreeable fame'.

Hell Fire Club members, perhaps, would have accepted that. 'We did what we liked – and we don't mind paying for it'.

Chapter 10

Gunpowder, Treason and Plot

'Please to remember the Fifth of November,
Gunpowder Treason and Plot.
We know no reason why gunpowder treason
Should ever be forgot'.

No one knows who wrote this little verse. It has been traditional since the 17th century. It refers of course to the Gunpowder Plot of 1605 when Guy Fawkes tried and failed to blow up Parliament and the king with it. The story was to have a sequel. There would be another plot too – the Rye House Plot of 1683.

Both plots had a common aim, to eliminate the king. But the two plots had conflicting motives. The instigators in 1605 were Catholics who wanted to destroy James I together with Parliament, as a prelude to a Catholic uprising. They failed.

The instigators in 1683 were largely surviving elements of Cromwell supporters who wanted to reverse the restoration of the Stuart monarchy which had taken place in 1660. It was a Protestant plot aimed at destroying both King Charles II and his brother, the future James II. It failed.

It is curious that in both plots all four of our shires come into the story, either geographically or through the personalities involved.

Sir Everard Digby of Gayhurst Manor in Buckinghamshire, and Robert Catesby of Ashby St. Ledger in Northamptonshire, were both deeply involved. Much of the working out of the details of the plot was done at Gayhurst and at Ashby.

Everard Digby was a Catholic and Catholics were subject to

Gayhurst Manor where the Gunpowder Plot was hatched. (NK)

harsh laws against Catholicism and the harbouring of Catholic priests. Digby had recently acquired Gayhurst Manor by marriage and in 1597 he was busily engaged in rebuilding the house. This gave him the opportunity of incorporating in the building both a secret room where a priest could be hidden, and a discreet chapel where Mass could be said.

Less than three miles from Gayhurst was Tyringham Manor. Robert Catesby of Ashby St. Ledger was a kinsman by marriage of the Tyringham family, and was also an ardent Catholic. Digby and Catesby were friends and the latter often visited Gayhurst.

To Gayhurst also came Guy Fawkes, and the plot was hatched to blow up Parliament and the king with it. Other secret meetings to the same end took place from time to time in a room over the gateway leading to the Manor House at Ashby St. Ledger.

The hope was that the success of the plot would give the signal for a Catholic uprising leading to the restoration of this country to the Catholic faith.

The plot was betrayed – ironically by another Northamptonshire Catholic, Francis Tresham of Rushton. So, on the morning of November 5th 1605 Guy Fawkes was caught red-handed in a cellar under Parliament before he had time to light the fuse to explode the thirty-six barrels of gunpowder that had been assembled there.

Digby's role in the plot was that under the guise of organising a hunting party in Worcestershire he would be in place to help promote the hoped-for Catholic uprising in the countryside. He was also expected to seize Elizabeth, the king's daughter, who was thought to be at a country house nearby.

Catesby's job was meant to be one of liaison – he would ride from London to give the news that the plot had succeeded. In the event, he had the opposite news to carry – the dire news that the plot had failed and that Guy Fawkes had been arrested.

For a few frenetic hours Digby entertained the mad hope that in spite of the failure of the plot in London, Catholics in the west might still rise. But he soon realised that this was a forlorn hope. So he intended to surrender himself to the Sheriff of Warwick. Before he could do so he was arrested by the Sheriff of Worcester. Meanwhile Catesby was shot trying to resist arrest.

On January 30th 1606 Sir Everard Digby, having been tried and condemned, was dragged through the street of London on a hurdle to St. Paul's Churchyard where he was hanged, drawn and quartered.

James I, the first monarch of the House of Stuart, had survived. He ruled for a further twenty-three years. In 1625 he was succeeded by his son Charles I whose reign saw the Civil War which ended in his execution in 1649.

Charles I who lost the Civil War.

The Commonwealth

Then came the eleven year rule of the Puritan, Oliver Cromwell, presiding over a republican England. It was a time when the Book of Common Prayer was proscribed, the observance of Christmas Day was abolished, all travel on Sunday was forbidden, all Catholic priests were hunted down or fled the country. Anglican clergy were forbidden to preach or teach. Many of them were ejected from their parishes and replaced by Puritan ministers. The press was censured

Oliver Cromwell who won the Civil War.

and a whole plethora of Puritan laws were imposed on every aspect of daily life. For the time being at least the great 'Elizabethan Settlement' was no more.

Elizabeth I in her long reign had tried with great skill to steer a middle course, avoiding the extreme Protestantism of Edward VI's reign and the rigid Catholicism of Mary I's reign. Both those two short reigns had led to many martyrs on both sides. Elizabeth's great settlement aimed at, and largely achieved a middle way which satisfied the great majority of the population. The trouble was it did not satisfy the die-hard Catholics on one side, or the Puritans on the other.

The abortive Gunpowder Plot failed to achieve Catholic aims. The eleven years of the Commonwealth under Cromwell saw Puritans in the ascendancy, but this was reversed by the restoration of the monarchy under Charles II. The next trial of strength came in 1683 in the Rye House Plot. This was an attempt by Puritans and Cromwellian survivors. If Buckinghamshire and Northamptonshire had been engaged in the Gunpowder Plot of 1605, it was Hertfordshire and Bedfordshire that figured in the Rye House Plot of 1683.

The Rye House Plot

The plot took its name from Rye House, the home of Rombold at Hoddeston in Hertfordshire. Rombold was a die-hard Cromwellian who bitterly regretted that Cromwell had been overthrown. Far from sharing the general rejoicing when the Stuart monarchy was restored under Charles II, Rombold feared that from a Protestant point of view things would become even worse when Charles would be succeeded by his brother James, the Duke of York. He suspected, with good reason, that Charles was a 'closet' Catholic, and he knew that James was a self-avowed Catholic.

So a number of people who shared Rombold's views gathered round him to discuss what they could do to strike a blow for the Protestant cause. Their number included other surviving Cromwellians like Rombold, and some extreme Whigs. This odd name came into use in the 17th century as a sort of nickname for those who regarded themselves as the champions of parliamentary supremacy and of toleration for Nonconformists. Whigs, therefore, were the political opponents of the Tory party which supported the monarchy and the Church.

The plot hatched was a simple one. King Charles II was at Newmarket together with his brother, the future James II. The plan was to murder them both on their journey back to London when they passed through Hoddeston. The simple plan failed for the simplest of reasons – the royal party left Newmarket earlier than expected, and had safely passed through Hoddeston before the plotters woke up to the fact.

The plot was uncovered. Arrests were made and trials followed. It was in those trials that Bedford became involved, because one of those tried, condemned and executed was Lord William Russell, the son of the Duke of Bedford.

William Russell was a leading Whig statesman who shared the views of those who plotted at Rye House. He felt strongly that the Duke of York, James, King Charles II's brother, being an avowed Catholic, must be prevented from succeeding to the throne. To this end he carried an Exclusion Bill up to the House of Lords. The Bill failed and the Duke of York went on to become King James II.

In the treason trials following the Rye House Plot many believed that the jury was packed and that some of the evidence put forward was spurious. The execution of William Russell was claimed by some as judicial murder.

So the two great plots in the 17th century both failed – the Gunpowder Plot of 1605 instigated by the Catholics, and the Rye House Plot of 1683 instigated by Protestants. Neither brought about the deaths of the kings they were intended to kill.

The tug of war between Catholics and Protestants for the control of England was finally resolved in the 'Glorious Revolution' of 1688, for then the Catholic James II abdicated, and his daughter Mary, an Anglican married to William of Orange, came to the throne. (See Chapter 1.) So much of the great 'Elizabethan Settlement' was recovered.

Chapter 11

England's First Martyr

On their great roads, like the Watling Street, the Romans established 'staging posts' every twelve to fourteen miles, this being the distance armed foot soldiers could march in a day. Examples in our region are Durocobrivis (Dunstable), Magiovinium (Fenny Stratford) and Lactodorum (Towcester). They built larger centres too as garrison towns, like Luguvalium (Carlisle) and Cataractonium (Catterick). They also established 'coloniae', or civic centres, including Eboracum (York), Corinium (Cirencester) and Lindum (Lincoln). Such places often became capitals of provinces. **But out of them all there was only one** '*Municipium*' or Chartered City, and that was *Verulamium*, St. Albans.

Verulamium was a sizable place with a whole range of military, civic, commercial and domestic buildings. It was surrounded by a city wall. A principle feature was a great amphitheatre capable of seating 50,000 people and used for plays, pantomimes, and a range of spectator sports, including cockfighting.

There were religious buildings too, temples for pagan worship. But there was no Christian church for Christianity was proscribed and Christians were persecuted. But there must have been a tiny number of Christians for there was a Christian priest. His name was Amphibalus and he was hunted and on the run.

He took refuge in the house of a soldier. That soldier was Alban, a man of Romano-British stock serving in the Roman army. Alban gave shelter to the fugitive priest. How long they

The Martyrdom of St. Alban – a 13th century drawing.

were together is not known, but it was long enough for Alban to be converted by Amphibalus and to become a Christian.

The authorities continued their search for the fugitive priest. When they came at last to the house where he was sheltering Alban changed clothes with Amphibalus, so it was he who was arrested and dragged off. He was taken along the causeway across the Ver to a hill top and there he was put to death. So died England's first martyr. The date was probably around 300. Tradition says that Amphibalus himself was subsequently caught and also put to death.

In 313 the Emperor Constantine, by the Edict of Milan, gave civil rights and toleration to Christians throughout the Roman Empire. At Verulamium a little church was built on the site of Alban's martyrdom. A visitor, Germanus, from Auxerre in France visited the little church in 429 and carried home what he believed to be blood-stained earth as a relic. The veneration of Alban had clearly begun.

King Offa of Mercia founded a monastery on the site of the martyrdom in 793 and Verulam's name was changed to St. Albans. By the time the Normans came in the 11th century the original monastery had fallen into ruins. It was replaced by a magnificent new Abbey, largely built by Abbot Paul of Caen (1077–1093). From the old Roman city, long since in ruins, bricks and stones were brought and used in the building of the new church. They can still be seen today, especially in the tower. Stone columns were also brought from the Saxon church built by Offa, and some ancient tiling also from the same place.

Abbot Paul's building survived as an Abbey until the dissolution of the monasteries at the Reformation. In 1539 it became a parish church. In 1875 it assumed the status of a Cathedral when St. Albans became a separate diocese. Its

St. Albans Abbey today.

length, 550 feet, is exceeded only by Winchester Cathedral, and St. Albans Cathedral stands higher above sea level than any other.

The Shrine of Saint Alban drew pilgrims in great numbers. When Danish invasions increased both in numbers and severity the monks transferred Alban's body to Ely lest it be desecrated by the Danes. When the Danish threat ceased the monks of Ely refused to return the body. But the monks of St. Albans then said they had only sent a duplicate body to Ely, and that the original body was still safely in their shrine! So there were then two rival shrines, at St. Albans and at Ely. Both sets of remains, genuine and spurious, were destroyed by Henry VIII. In the 19th century the shrine at St. Albans was reconstructed from pieces of the old shrine which Henry VIII had ordered to be destroyed.

The earliest complete account we have of Alban's martyrdom is that given by Bede who in 731 completed his great work: 'The Ecclesiastical History of the English people'. Allowing for the propensity of writers at that early date to accept as natural events which later generations would be tempted to discount as naïve or superstitious, here is how Bede wrote of England's first martyr:

A priest flying for his life in time of persecution came to the house of Alban, then a pagan and was given shelter, and converted his host to Christianity by his life and teaching. The pursuers, having traced their fugitive, appeared at Alban's house and demanded his surrender. Alban put on the other's clothes, gave himself up and was led before the judges, who ordered him to renounce his Christianity. Alban refused. Then said the judge: 'Of what family or race are you?' 'What does it concern you of what stock I am?' was the answer. 'If you desire to hear the truth of my religion, be it known to you that I am now a Christian and bound by Christian duties'. 'I ask your name' said the judge, 'tell it me immediately'. 'I am called Alban by my parents, and I worship and adore the true and living God who created all things'. The judge, infuriated, ordered him to sacrifice. Alban refused, and he was ordered to be scourged. Then finding him to be still obdurate the judge sentenced him to be beheaded.

On the way to the execution there was a river, the bridge over which was so crowded with spectators that his procession could not get by. In answer to his prayer, the stream is said to have dried up. On their arrival at the hill on which the execution was to take place, he prayed for water, and a spring broke out under his feet. His executioner was so moved that he threw down his sword, fell at Alban's feet, and refused to execute his office. Another soldier was called upon, and both perished together.

Bede adds that a church of suitable dignity was built on the site of the martyrdom, on what is known as Holy Well Hill.

Chapter 12

How Very Odd !

In the days when Amersham on the southern slops of the Chiltern Hills was a tiny place with very few voters it nevertheless regularly returned two members to Parliament. It did so from 1624 right up to the Reform Act of 1832. Sir William Drake built the Market Hall in 1682 and it bears his coat of arms. The parish church contains several monuments to succeeding members of the Drake family which owned the property and house of Shardeloes. It was in about 1605 that Joan Tothill of Shardeloes married Francis Drake of Esher. This marked the beginning of the Buckinghamshire Drake family. *Joan was the eldest of thirty-three children!*

Farnham Royal on the upper slopes of the Thames valley was given after the Conquest to Bertrand de Verdon on one condition: *he was to provide a glove and put it on the king's right hand at the coronation, and to support the king's right hand while the newly-crowned monarch held the royal sceptre.* It is for this reason that Farnham has the suffix 'Royal'.

Take the Northampton road out of Olney for about two miles and then turn left into Yardley Chase and you will come to the old hollow oak immortalised by William Cowper in his poem 'The Task', published in 1785. In Cowper's time the oak was known as Judith but he called it the Yardley Oak. He took the trouble to records its dimensions in his day – twenty-eight feet five inches in girth. By the beginning of this century its girth had increased to over thirty-two feet. Near to Judith stood another great and ancient tree. The two became known as Gog and Magog.

When Sir Toby Belch is trying to persuade Sir Andrew Aguecheek in Twelfth Night to issue a challenge to the supposed youth Cesario (who is really Viola in disguise) he urges him to write a fierce letter and to fill it with 'as many lies as will lie in thy sheet of paper although the sheet were big enough *for the bed of Ware in England'*. There really was such a bed. It was made in the 16th century and was huge – a four-poster bed eleven feet square and capable of holding twelve people. It used to be at Rye House in Hertfordshire but in 1931 it came into the possession of the Victoria and Albert Museum.

In 1868 the Charity Commissioners were asked to vary the terms of a Bequest called the Bell Rope Charity. Under this Bequest money had been left in trust for the purchase of bell ropes for the church in Stony Stratford. It came about because centuries before a traveller had been lost at night in Whittlewood Forest. He feared for his life but was rescued from his panic when in the distance he heard the church bells of Stony Stratford and was able to make his way towards the sound. So he was saved by the bell! In gratitude he left money to the town to keep the bell ropes in good repair so that the bells would continue to ring. The interest from the Trust proved more than was needed for the purpose, so the Charity Commissioners were asked, and agreed, that the money could be put instead towards insurance of the church against fire.

Northamptonshire has a nice companion story to this. It concerns Weldon. In this instance too a traveller was lost deep in the forest – Rockingham Forest this time. After wandering in panic for some time the traveller spotted the tower of Weldon Church. In relief and gratitude he left money to pay for a lantern to be placed at the top of the tower to help other travellers. The lantern is still there. So could Weldon Church tower be the most inland lighthouse in the country?

Here are three odd stories in stone. The oldest concerns the Soulbury Boulder between Bletchley and Wing in Buckinghamshire. Folk lore says it rolled into the village of its own volition. Perhaps in a sense it did. It is what the experts call a 'glacial erratic' which originated millions of years ago in Derbyshire and was stranded in Soulbury at the end of the Ice Age.

No less odd is puddingstone found in fields in and around the Chilterns. Puddingstone comprises glacial conglomerates of

The Soulbury Boulder, left over from the Ice Age millions of years ago. (JH)

flint pebbles. It somewhat resembles bread pudding in appearance and is sometimes used in church buildings, as at Great Munden in Hertfordshire. Puddingstone was once highly prized for its magical properties, useful for warding off evil spirits. Perhaps that is why it was used in the walls of churches.

But most of all it was venerated because it was said to be able to reproduce itself underground, which is why it is sometimes called 'breeding stone'. Pebbles were believed to grow into large boulders below ground.

To complete this trio of stories in stone there is the fact that at Aspley Guise chemical properties in the soil can cause wood to petrify. Celia Fiennes in her diary written three hundred years ago made this entry: *'I went to Asply (Aspley Guise) where the earth turns wood into stone and had a piece of it. It seemes its only one sort of wood, the alder tree, which turns so. Lay or drive a paille or stake into the ground there, in seven years its petrified into stone'.*

Both Northamptonshire and Buckinghamshire have tales of how the choice of sites for building or rebuilding churches was interfered with by unearthly forces.

In 1325 it was decided to rebuild Olney Church on a new site, but on four nights in a row building materials assembled on the proposed site were mysteriously moved after dark to another site. *'Happily it was perceived that this occurrence could be none other than a message from Heaven and it was therefore proposed to build the church on the ground thus miraculously indicated'.*

At West Wycombe the church was originally intended to stand at the foot of a hill. *'But as fast as a portion of the building was erected it was removed during the night by some invisible agency which deposited the materials at the top of the hill'.* The folk lore goes on to relate that when a priest was summoned with bell, book and candle to exorcise the site *'a weird unearthly voice promised to abstain from further annoyance if the church should be erected upon the spot to which the materials had been removed. This being done the work proceeded without further interruption'.*

A very similar tale relates to Wendover Church. When the building started *'the materials were all carried away by witches and deposited where the church now stands'*. The field where it had been intended to erect the church is still called Witchall Meadow.

If the Olney folk tried four times to resist the interference by these unknown forces, the people of Stowe were made of sterner stuff. They had their building materials moved *nine* times, and nine times they carried them back. They then set a man to watch at night to see who or what was moving the materials. But his report was so vague and unsatisfactory that they could make neither head nor tail of it. So in the end they built the church on the site to which the materials been carried.

Here is a tale that was made famous as long ago as the 16th century by Thomas Deloney who included it in his 'Historie of Thomas of Reading'. It tells of the gruesome behaviour of a couple named Jarman who in medieval times kept the old Ostrich Inn at Colnbrook. They had a technique which Sweeney Todd would have admired. They murdered rich travellers by putting them in a bed fixed to a trap door. When the trapdoor was activated the occupant of the bed fell into a cauldron of boiling ale in the kitchen below!

An unfortunate clothier from Reading was their sixtieth victim. His name was Thomas Cole. According to Deloney it is Cole who gives Colnbrook its name. And he also claims that it is this same Cole who is celebrated in the nursery rhyme, 'Old King Cole'.

Some *Young* Traditions

Traditions do not always go back for hundreds of years. Two examples of 'young' traditions are furnished by Little Horwood and Ashendon in Buckinghamshire.

Little Horwood was the site of a World War II airfield from 1942 to 1946. In those years it was a hive of activity. After 1946 the quiet of a small village returned. In 1968 it was decided to launch a Social Amenities Association to give new life to the village. Ever since then the Association has developed a number of initiatives and annual events.

Perhaps the oddest of all is the Annual Duck Race held on Boxing Day. The ducks, sporting knitted colours round their necks, are raced in the brook. As well as being a fun event, the Boxing Day Duck Race raises money for the recreation ground in the village.

Ashendon's 'young' tradition goes back to 1962. The broken gate to the Allotments had lain in the hedge for years. In 1962 it was repaired and rehung by two public-minded villagers. To mark the occasion a public Dinner was organised! So a tradition was born. The Annual Gatehangers Dinner still goes on. The money it raises is used for a variety of good causes in Ashendon.

Chapter 13

A Fence Taken

There was no other word for it but 'mania'. Railway mania gripped the country just as, earlier, Canal mania had done. For the canals landowners, speculators and engineers had schemed and competed. Now it was the turn of yet other landowners, speculators and engineers to engage in a mad race to get rich quick. All over the country meetings were held and new Railway Companies were launched. They competed with each other, but they also competed with landowners who opposed railway construction.

Prominent in the anti-railway lobby was the Duke of Buckingham, determined to keep the railways from spreading over his land. Of the many new lines projected there was one he particularly opposed. It would have brought the detested tracks through his property at Stowe. He knew that before tracks could be laid surveys must be carried out. So he gathered his labourers and dependants together and organised them into vigilantes. They were to chase off any surveyors who turned up, and if a few heads were cracked in the process, no questions would be asked.

But the surveyors were under pressure too. The companies set up to open new lines had invested good money and they wanted a return on their investment. An Irish engineer named Byrne was charged with the task of surveying the lands round Stowe, and he had his team of surveyors.

So the battle was joined – the Duke's posse of labourers armed with their sticks, and the engineers armed with their theodolites. Quite a few pitched battles took place as surveyors and chainmen were confronted by resolute farm labourers. Cunning was employed by both sides. For the Duke, the obvious strategy was to make it impossible for the surveyors to use their theodolites. If they couldn't be physically hounded off the land, at least they must somehow be prevented from taking their levels. So large sheets and tarpaulins were brought into play. They were erected on poles and stretched across fields and roads, denying theodolite reading.

But the engineers could be cunning too. Their strategy was twofold. First, they decided to make their survey by moonlight, figuring that labourers who had worked all day would be unlikely to be on the alert all night too. Second, the engineers divided into two teams. One team of surveyors and chainmen made a great show of activity in one area of the Duke's property, while a second team quietly went to work in another area. In that second area Byrne's men arrived with two ladders which they erected on a footpath fifty yards apart. That gave them a base-line. By taking their theodolite readings from the ladders, they achieved their levels by sighting over the top of the obstructing tarpaulins. In this way, moving the ladders laboriously from place to place they succeeded in one tiring moonlit night in surveying a crucial half mile of levels.

So one after another Railway companies were formed and plans were made for submission to Government. In each case an Act of Parliament would be needed. Government Regulations set a date as a deadline by which the plans must be submitted.

November 30th 1847 was one such date. By midnight on that day all plans must be submitted. Throughout that day the White Hart in Aylesbury was swarming with engineers, lawyers, Parliamentary agents, and landowners or their representatives. There was a frantic last minute rush not only to get each batch of plans assembled and rolled up, but also to get them delivered to the right places by midnight. It was a complicated affair. By midnight the separate batches of plans must be handed in at places as diverse as Oxford, Reading, Hertford, Bedford and Northampton. Throughout the day post-chaises left at intervals from the yard at the White Hart in Aylesbury and sped off with the precious batches of plans.

By evening all the batches but one were on their way. The one exception was the batch of plans for the Midland Grand Junction Line which was intended to run from Northampton to Reading. Vital parts of the plan were still awaited. As the hours passed there was much clock-watching and nail biting.

It was almost 8pm before the Northampton plans were ready. For some time an engine with steam up had been waiting at Aylesbury Station. Attached to the engine was a single coach and the guard's brake van. At last two clerks with the precious plans rushed to the Station and boarded the train. They had fifty miles to cover to Northampton. Could they do it in time? The mad rush began.

Between Leighton Buzzard and Bletchley disaster struck – the fuel on the train was exhausted. Frantically the guard and the clerks jumped down from the train. They tore up the rails of the fence alongside the track and broke them up to fuel the engine. They managed to keep the fire in the engine going until the train reached Bletchley where more adequate supplies of fuel were available. But a vital half-hour had been lost. Could they reach Northampton by midnight? It look doubtful.

In the event it was a quarter to twelve when they pulled up in Northampton. The two clerks leapt from the train and rushed off up the steep hill to the Office of the Clerk of the Peace on Market Square. Breathless, they banged on the door just before the clock in the nearby All Saints Church struck midnight.

But no-one answered their knock! A policeman then appeared. He told them that the Clerk of the Peace had gone home and had left word that the plans should be delivered to his house, five minutes distance away. Desperately they rushed there, only to be told that the plans could not be accepted because it was now after twelve o'clock! Indignantly they pointed out that they had been at the Office just *before* midnight, but the official was obdurate. All through this altercation the official's front door was open, so they simply threw the plans into the house and made their way back to the station. On board the little train once more they made their way safely back to Aylesbury, arriving there at 3am.

Two further details complete this tale. The first is that it took a meeting of the Government's Standing Order Committee to determine whether the plans had been delivered before the deadline. Standing Committee decreed that they had been, accepting the testimony of the Policeman who had directed them to the house of the Clerk of the Peace.

The second remaining detail concerns the irate farmer whose fence had been ripped up between Leighton Buzzard and Bletchley. They listened to his complaint and tried to pacify him. 'No offence intended' they said. 'Maybe not' he answered, 'but a fence was taken!' It would be nice to think he was suitable recompensed – for his pun as well as for his property!

Chapter 14

Affairs of the Heart

In 1833 two brothers, William and Robert Chambers, began the publication of The Edinburgh Journal. As one would expect, their writings were almost exclusively about matters Scottish. But one of their publications, 'A Book of Days', for some reason paid particular attention to Buckinghamshire. They also had a strange preoccupation with matters to do with the heart, though not in the usual romantic context of such a subject. Here are some extracts from their book, written well over one hundred years ago in Scotland:

'Some curious notions and practices respecting the human heart came into vogue about the time of the first Crusade. The heart was considered the most valuable of all legacies, and it became the habit of a person to bequeath it to his dearest friend, or to his most favourite church, abbey or locality, as a token of his supreme regard. The hearts would be carefully embalmed, enclosing them in some costly casket. This remarkable practice was most prevalent during the medieval ages.'

The Chambers brothers then went on to itemise their subject, with particular reference to Buckinghamshire:

'Sir Robert Peckham, who died abroad, caused his heart to be sent into England and buried in his family vault at Denham. He died in 1569, but his heart appears to have remained unburied as we gather from the following entry in the parish register of burials: "Edmundus Peckham, Esq., July 18, 1586. On the same day was the harte of Sir Robt Peckham buried in the vault under the chappell".'

'Edward Lord Windsor of Bradenham, who died at Spa,

January 24, 1574 bequeathed his body to be buried in "the cathedral church of the noble city of Liege, but his heart to be enclosed in lead and sent into England, there to be buried in the chapel at Bradenham under his father's tomb, in token of a true Englishman". The case containing this heart is still in the vault at Bradenham and was seen in 1848 when Isaac d'Israeli was buried in the same vault.'

'The Book of Days' then moved away from historical fact into the realm of popular folk lore:

'It may be just noticed in passing . . . that formerly the executioner of a traitor was required to remove the body from the gallows before life was extinct, and plucking out the heart to hold it up in his hands and exclaim aloud: "Here is the heart of a traitor!" When the executioner held up the heart of Sir Everard Digby of Gayhurst Sir Everard made answer and said "Thou liest!". Lord Bacon affirms that there are instances of persons saying two or three words in similar cases.'

Finally the writers return to historical fact again:

'On a brass in the church of Lillingstone Dayrell the heart is inscribed with the letters J.H.C. and is held in two hands cut off at the wrist. This heart commemorates the interment of John Merton, Rector, who died in 1486.'

The Chambers brothers might have included a further example from Buckinghamshire if they had known about it. It concerns Paul Whitehead (1710–1784). He was an English satirist and minor poet, son of a tailor, who married an imbecile with a fortune of £10,000. He spent some years in the Fleet Prison for debt, and later became active in politics. He was one of the infamous 'monks' of Medmenham (see Chapter 9) and became deputy treasurer of the Hell Fire Club. West Wycombe Church contains Paul Whitehead's heart which had been bequeathed to Sir Francis Dashwood, the founder of the Hell Fire Club. Sir Francis arranged for the heart to be interred with full military honours.

But Buckinghamshire does not have a total monopoly on this subject of hearts and their burial. Northamptonshire too has a heart story to tell. Woodford Church on the banks of the

River Nene contains a human heart which can be seen through a small window high up in the fourth pillar of the north aisle. Whose heart was it, and how did it come to be deposited in Woodford Church? These are mysteries. Some say it is the heart of Sir Walter Trayli whose carved wooden effigy with that of his wife can be seen at the end of the chancel. Sir Walter Trayli died in the Levant at the end of the last Crusade in 1290. It is said that while he was buried abroad, his heart was sent back to England. This accords well with the observations made by the Chambers brothers and quoted above. But why was the heart buried in the pillar and not in the tomb with Sir Walter's wife?

Chapter 15

Not Many People Know That !

That was the title Michael Caine gave to a paperback he wrote about ten years ago. It became a best-seller. Its subtitle was 'An Almanac of Amazing Facts'.

It would be idle to suppose that what follows in this chapter will amaze anybody. But perhaps it contains some things of which it can be said: 'Not many people know that!'. See what you think.

The Chiltern Hundreds

Ever since 1750 it has been impossible for an MP to resign his seat between General Elections. But what such an MP can do is to apply for the job of Steward of the Chiltern Hundreds. The Hundreds in question are Stoke, Desborough, and Burnham.

Originally the Steward's job there was a tough one – he was expected to suppress the robbers who frequented the thickly-wooded Chiltern Hills. The Stewardship today is just a quaint but useful device to enable an MP to resign his seat in Parliament in mid-term. But he will need to be nominated by the Chancellor of the Exchequer in whose gift the Chiltern Hundreds are.

The Peer and The Bible

On April 24th 1693 Lord Wharton issued this instruction:

'1050 Bibles with the singing psalms bound up therewith, and the like number of catechisms, should be yearly provided, and there

should be a printed paper pasted inside the Bible to this effect: "Those reading psalms in the English translation in the Bible are to be learnt without Book, by the child to whom this book is presented, namely the 1st, 15th, 37th, 101st, 113th and 145th." The reward to be given to such children who can read, or poor people, of good report in the Cities, Towns, and Places therein named, in Yorkshire, Westmoreland, Cumberland, and Buckinghamshire – in the latter county namely in Winslow 10, Aylesbury 20, Wendover 10, Amersham 10, Chesham 10, Chipping Wycombe 10, Great Marlow 10, Beaconsfield 10, Wooburn 10, Winchendon and Waddeston 10; and that on the day of the delivery of the Bibles there should be sermons preached, for which 10/- is allowed at such places as are therein named, the purport, design, and scope of every such sermon to be to discover and prove to the people the truth, usefulness, sufficiency, and excellence of the Holy Scriptures, and the people's right to have them fully in their own language; and also their duty to read, study, and search the Scriptures, and take them for their only unerring rule of faith, worship, and manners.'

Lord Wharton was a Whig statesmen. He was forty-five when the 'Lord Wharton's Bibles' scheme was launched. He went on fifteen years later to become Lord-Lieutenant of Ireland. He was a fervent Protestant and is remembered also as the author of the satirical anti-catholic ballad 'Lilliburlelo'.

Church Registers and the Law

In 1653 the Government under Cromwell passed a Law saying that henceforth Church Registers should only record the births of children and not their baptisms. The aim was to eliminate the baptism of infants. The law was opposed and ignored by many parish priests.

Among them was Matthew Bate, the Vicar of Maids Moreton near Buckingham. He told his parishioners forthrightly that any child entered in his Parish Register would certainly have been baptised.

The Puritan Government, as well as seeking to discourage

infant baptism, also sought to secularise marriage. They enacted that henceforth marriage must be performed, not by the priest, but by the Justice of the Peace. Here again, Matthew Bate of Maids Moreton gave the new law short shrift. He announced stoutly: 'None of this parish are bedded before they are solemnly wedded in the Church, and that according to the Order of the Church of England'.

Happily such interferences with ancient Church Order came to an end when Cromwell was overthrown and the monarchy was restored under Charles II in 1660.

The Wool Trade

In 1667 an Act was passed in Parliament making it compulsory for every corpse to be buried in a woollen shroud. The aim was to encourage the Wool Trade! There was an escape clause. Those who wished could bury their dead in linen, but must pay a fine in consequence. That 1667 Act was not removed from the Statute Book until 1814. But no doubt it had been quietly ignored long before that. From 1840 onwards Leighton Buzzard had the largest Wool Fair in Buckinghamshire. At the Wool Fair in 1840 some 140 farmers sold 30,000 fleeces.

The 1667 Act was not the first time that Government issued a regulation which, while it purported to be a religious instruction, also had a secondary motive to promote a trade or commercial concern. In 1558 an Act was passed ordering abstinence from flesh meat on all days formerly accounted fasting days. The Act said it was 'for the better subduing of the body to the soul'. But it also added that it was for the 'encouragement of mariners and the increase of shipping'. In other words, eat more fish and less meat!

Stamp Duty

In 1783 a Stamp Duty was introduced on births and burials. A Duty of 3d was levied on every entry in the Church Registers relating to births and burials. The only exception was for the birth or burial of a pauper. In those cases the word 'Pauper' had to be written as part of the entry in the Registers. The duty was repealed in 1794.

Barn Preachers

A Vicar in June 1908 found some puzzling entries in his old Church Register. They included:

'June 22, 1703 Jane, wife of Richard Hayward, Yeoman, was interred by Mr Patterson, a BARN PREACHER.

'December 12, 1705 Elenora Hunt, widow, was interred by Mr Patterson, a BARN PREACHER.

'October 13, 1706 a son of Jn Rakestraw, Day Labourer, was born and named James by Mr Phillips, a BARN PREACHER.'

The vicar wondered: 'Were these Barn Preachers itinerating or resident? Ordained or unordained? And how came they in the early part of the 18th century to be allowed to officiate?'

It was William Bradbrook, author of The History of Fenny Stratford, who offered an answer. He wrote:

Sir,

Dr Wood enquires about certain entries in the parish register which mention 'a Barn Preacher'. It will be noted that all the examples quoted by him occur in the early part of the 18th century, and during the Wars in Flanders. To help carry on these wars a tax was imposed on every register entry, or rather on every birth or baptism, marriage and burial, and this tax had to be collected by the Incumbent. As schism was far from uncommon,

NOT MANY PEOPLE
KNOW THAT!

many people escaped entry in the parish register during ordinary times, but when a tax had to be paid, registration became compulsory. Probably the parson had to look up defaulters and enter them for the sake of the tax, and the words 'by a Barn Preacher' indicate that the religious observance was either nil or irregular. The entries quoted by Dr Wood which deal with births, state that the infant was named, not baptised.

Yours &c.,

W Bradbrook

Bletchley, 9th July 1908

Chapter 16

Highways and Byways

'Before the Roman came to Rye, or out to Severn strode, the rolling English drunkard made the rolling English road.'

Perhaps 'drunkard' was a bit unkind. But Chesterton was right. There were indeed English roads in this land long before the Romans came. They grew slowly, over centuries, and none of them were the planned, designed routes such as the Romans were to make.

The Ridgeway, some eighty-five miles in length, became, over time, a broad track running along the top of chalk downland ridges. It started to the southwest of our region, passing through Wiltshire, Oxfordshire and Berkshire. It crossed the Thames near Goring into Buckinghamshire, traversed the Chiltern Hills, and entered Hertfordshire over Pitstone Hill near Ivinghoe Beacon. Along its length are signs of our ancient history – burial mounds, Iron-age forts, images cut in chalk on the hills, and those strange stone circles – all these speak of our ancient past.

That ancient road, The Ridgeway, is perhaps four or five thousand years old. Over it, for centuries, men have walked driving their sheep and cattle. It evolved. It wasn't planned or constructed – it just happened. In place of the direct, straight-line precision that the Romans were to bring to their roads, the ancient English roads meandered and wandered, always seeking the high ground and avoiding the mud and swamps of lower down.

The Icknield Way was its other name, so called from the Iceni, the Celtic tribe who inhabited East Anglia. It made possible the two-way traffic of those early centuries – the corn and cattle of the east, and the mineral wealth of the southwest.

There was also the Akeman Street, entering Buckinghamshire near Tring and passing through Aston Clinton to Bicester. it is not certain that this was an entirely separate road. Perhaps it was a more northerly branch of the Icknield Way. Even less certain is how it got its name. It has been said that Akeman Street was so called because along this road 'aching men' passed, seeking the benefit of the waters of Bath (Aquae Sulis). Improbable though that may sound, it has to be added that one of the Saxon names for Bath was 'Akemannes-ceaster', or 'the city of invalids'.

Finally there was the Fosse Way, running from Lincoln down to Cornwall. It, or a branch of it, ran between Stony Stratford and Water Stratford in Buckinghamshire. Though there is little evidence of this today, it can hardly be a coincidence that between these two places lies Foscote – whose name implies that it was originally a village or hamlet on the Fosse Way.

If the 'rolling English roads' of the past were the haphazard creation of centuries, the roads the Romans built were of a different order. They were deliberate, planned, and utilitarian – useful tools of military occupation and civil administration.

In the great web of roads which the Romans constructed, the three most important were those that fanned out of London – one to the north through York to the borders of Scotland; another through Gloucester to the west; and the third through St. Albans to Chester and on from there to Carlisle. That third road is our Watling Street, traversing each of our four shires.

Watling Street began as a great Roman road, perhaps the most important of all the Roman roads; it continued as a great coaching road. The Canals, when they came, were constructed in large measure parallel to it. So, over the centuries, first, Roman legionaries; then great passenger and mail coaches; then canals with their barges; and then railways carrying both freight and passengers. All have found their way through our

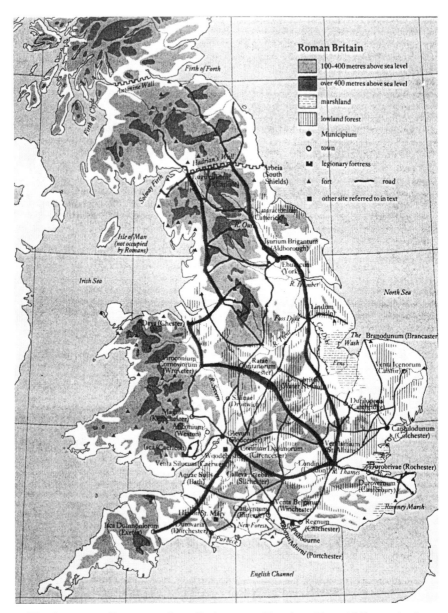

The three great Roman roads radiating out of London. The middle one is the
Watling Street – the 'great northwest diagonal' on which lie our four shires.

four shires on the great north-west diagonal fanning out from London. Finally, following that same route, the series was completed with the construction of Britain's first Motorway, the M1. It too passes through each of our four shires.

Perhaps the most interesting place in this context is Dunstable. For there two great roads crossed – our ancient English Icknield Way and the Roman Watling Street. Nearby are the remains both of a Roman Camp and of a British Stronghold.

Where the two roads met was the spot chosen by King Edward I for the erection of an Eleanor Cross in 1290, for the body of his dead queen, Eleanor, rested for a night in Dunstable Abbey as the funeral cortege made its way to Westminster. Alas, Dunstable's Eleanor Cross did not survive the Civil War in the 17th century. But the record tells us that where the ancient Icknield Way met the Roman Watling Street, there the Prior of Dunstable Abbey received the body of the Queen and, having sprinkled the crossroads with Holy Water, he bore her body into his Abbey to rest overnight in state.

It is one thing to build a great road system, it is quite another to find the finance to maintain it. In this last decade of the twentieth century we grow more and more conscious of that fact. Tolls are seen as one answer to the problem. The answer is not new. Tolls were widely introduced long ago.

It had early been found unsatisfactory to make towns and parishes responsible for the maintenance of the roads that passed through them. They had neither the skill nor the resources to cope. So by Act of Parliament Trusts were authorised, empowering the Trustees to raise money by loan to improve the highways, and authorising the Trustees to recoup their outlay by charging tolls to be paid by road-users. And that meant Turnpike Gates, erected across the road and opened by Turnpike Gatekeepers (or 'Pikers') only for those who had paid to go through. There was a Tariff – for a horse, ridden or led, one and a half pence; for any vehicle, four and a half pence.

Once the Toll was paid the payer was at liberty to go through the gate as often as he wished, up till midnight. Once

Dunstable Priory. Dunstable stands where the Watling Street and the Icknield Way crossed. At that crossing the body of Queen Eleanor was received and taken into the Abbey to rest overnight.

midnight struck, a further payment was required.

'Pikers' were a race apart. They could be affable or awkward, obliging or surly. Dickens makes the elder Sam Weller say of 'Pikers':

'They're all on 'em men as has met with some disappointment in life, consequence of vich they retires from the world and shuts themselves up in pikes, partly with the view of being solitary, and partly to revenge themselves on mankind by takin' tolls.'

How would Sam Weller describe Traffic Wardens, one wonders!

To all our towns on the Watling Street catering for coaches and travellers was both a way of life and a means of livelihood. The coaches carried both passengers and mail. Inn Signboards carried the important words: 'Posting House'. This meant that not only could horses be provided for the onward journey of the travellers, but that accommodation could also be offered for travellers and their servants. In return for the privilege of conducting such business, Innkeepers paid to the Government a heavy tax, called The Post-horse Duty. The duty was reckoned at one and a half pence per horse per mile.

There was great rivalry and competition for this business. In every important town there would be two rival Posting Houses. At one the Postboys rode in blue jackets, at the other in yellow jackets. And, whatever their age, they were all called Postboys. As Sam Weller once remarked: *Nobody ever saw a dead Postboy'.*

But how was the Post-horse Duty collected? Quite simply (!). At each stage, as the horses were being changed, the Innkeeper made out a ticket. The ticket bore the Royal Coat of Arms. There were blank spaces which had to be filled in: for the date; the place from which the horses had started; the place of destination; the number of miles to that destination; and the name of the driver. Each morning the Innkeeper had to fill up an official duty sheet, showing every hiring of the previous day, the number of miles, and the amount payable. (Shades of VAT Returns of a later age!)

Just a hundred years ago J K Fowler wrote three fascinating books: 'Echoes of Old Country Life', 'Recollections of Old

Country Life', and 'Records of Old Times'. In them he looked back on a long life. So, much of what he wrote dealt with events, for us, going back for the best part of two hundred years.

Writing of the old coaching days J K Fowler recounted an incident which his father had told him about. It happened on June 20th 1815. Mr Fowler, Senior, then aged twenty-three, was haymaking in his meadow that day. The coach, 'The Dairy Maid', pulled up alongside the field. Its driver called out: *'Master John, I bring you great news, and no one in Aylesbury shall know it before you. Boneyparte and all his French Army are destroyed! The Duke of Wellington, God bless him, has fought and beat him at a place called Waterloo.'*

So, writes J K Fowler,: *'My father hurried to the Parish Clerk to tell him to call the ringers together, and soon a peal of eight bells poured out a volume of sound which, as my father reported in great joy, was powerful enough to shake the steeple'.*

Chapter 17

Fire and Plague

It is hard to think of two greater disasters, other than war, that could afflict mankind in centuries past than fire and plague. No town or village escaped them. Yet there was one moment in history when these two scourges almost coincided, and in so doing proved beneficent. That was in the two succeeding years, 1665 and 1666. 1665 had seen the worst pestilence the country had known for centuries – the Great Plague. A year later, in 1666, occurred the worst conflagration the capital had ever seen – the Great Fire of London. Both were disasters on a massive scale, yet the effect of the Great Fire was, in a sense, to sanitise and disinfect the streets of stricken London. Perhaps those who survived the successive calamities were in no mood to count their blessings, but the fact remains that the Great Fire helped to snuff out the Great Plague which had preceded it.

The Black Death

The plague known as the Black Death was bubonic. It came from Asia and ravaged Europe between 1348 and 1351. It reached England in 1348 and carried off one-eighth of the population. It was called the Black Death because of the dark skin haemorrhage which accompanied it. It was spread by the bite of infected rat fleas. Because it was invariably accompanied by coughing and sneezing it is thought to have inspired the nursery rhyme:

> 'Ring a ring o'roses
> A pocket full of posies
> A-tishoo! A-tishoo!
> We all fall down'.

The 'ring o'roses' meant the red rash which was usually the first sign of the onset of the disease. The 'posies' were sweet-smelling flowers and herbs used to detract from the stench of the dead.

Though the years 1348–1351 saw the most calamitous death toll, there were also periodic visitations at intervals thereafter. London suffered again in 1361–1362, and in 1379. And finally, the worst visitation of all, the Great Plague of 1665.

This repetitive pattern was seen all over the country. Fenny Stratford, for example, suffered at least six serious outbreaks of plague between 1500 and 1665, with well over one hundred deaths in that latter year.

A St. Albans monk wrote of the 14th century Plague:

'Scarcely the half of mankind survived. Towns that were formely very thickly populated were left destitute of inhabitants, the plague being so violent that the living were scarce able to bury the dead'.

One bishop wrote:

'The contagious nature of the present pestilence, which is spreading itself far and wide, has left many parish churches, and consequently the people, destitute of curates and priests'.

He could have been describing the situation at Luton. There, first the Vicar died of the plague at the beginning of 1349. The priest sent to replace him died before the year was up. The next replacement was so scared that he ran away. By 1350 a clerk only in deacon's orders was all that could be found to take over the parish.

The Prior of St. Albans died of the Plague, along with forty-seven of his monks – three-quarters of the entire complement of the Abbey.

To escape the plague in London many fled to the countryside, which served to carry the infection still wider. A sad example of this concerns the tiny village of Gibraltar in Buckinghamshire. To escape the plague a group of Londoners walked all the way to the village, where one of their number had relatives. But they carried the infection with them, with the result that forty of Gibraltar's eighty inhabitants perished.

Markham wrote that the Black Death was 'at its fiercest in North Bucks. from May to September 1349. Half the clergy fell to it and the general population was almost halved. Mills were empty and farms left derelict'. Bradwell Priory suffered greatly, its Prior and many of the monks dying. The Priory buildings deteriorated for want of monks to care for them.

Not surprisingly, such epidemics filled people with terror. There was no cure. There were no hospitals – only 'Pest Houses' where an attempt could be made to isolate the infected. Even the clergy were sometimes too terrified to conduct funerals lest they be infected. In a later visitation Cole, the diarist/rector of Bletchley, went to conduct a funeral in a parish not his own because no other clergy would risk it.

The bubonic plagues were not the only intermittent scourge to afflict people. Cholera epidemics also exacted a fearful toll from time to time. Once more the little village of Gibraltar provides a sad example. Forty-eight people died there of Cholera in a few hours in 1849.

We turn now to that other kind of disaster – Fire. But before we do so the village of Bolnhurst in Bedfordshire provides an interesting link. There was a fire in Bolnhurst in 1665. But it was no accident. It destroyed most of the village, and it was started deliberately in a desperate attempt to stem the Great Plague.

Fire !
Just as many places experienced repeated outbreaks of plague, so, too, many places suffered repeated outbreaks of fire. Stony Stratford, for example, had major fires in 1703, 1725, 1736 and 1742. Woburn had at least three serious conflagrations. Luton had a major fire in 1336, and before it could recover from that, had another four years later in 1340. Olney has had innumerable fires, two of them major, in 1787 and 1854. Of many fires in Northampton's history the worst by far was that in 1675. This destroyed so much of the town that Charles II

awarded Northampton one thousand tons of timber from Whittlewood Forest to help with the rebuilding. In the list of Buckingham's many fires the worst by far was in 1725.

The sheer number of houses lost at each of these fires is staggering. It is not uncommon to read such statements as: 'half of the town was burnt down', or 'a third of the town was lost'. Even in a village the same could be true. In Great Horwood, for example, the toll of its fire in 1781 was sixteen farmhouses, four malt houses and forty cottages.

So the catalogue continues. Fifty-three houses in one Stony Stratford fire and a hundred and forty-six in another. One hundred and thirty houses lost in a day at Woburn. One hundred and thirty-eight houses destroyed in Buckingham. Fifty-five totally destroyed and twenty-five others seriously damaged at Olney.

Such statistics may appal us but they cannot surprise us. Houses were thatched. Many of them were made of timber, wattle and daub, not brick or stone. One roof on fire – and sparks from it could ignite a dozen others in a matter of minutes.

No organised fire services existed, or would exist, till much later. The most sophisticated aid available would be a long hooked pole for pulling the burning thatch to the ground. Such a pole, for communal use, might be kept at the church – as it was at Hanslope, where it can still be seen. By the time it could be fetched, half the village might be lost.

Sundial House in Stony Stratford has an attractive Sundial affixed to its wall. It bears the inscription:

TEMPUS ET IGNIS OMNIA PERDUNT

'Time and fire consume all things'. That has certainly been the case for all the many hundred of houses that have gone up in flames in past centuries in all our towns and villages. It says much for human resilience that new homes and houses have always risen, Phoenix-like, from their ashes.

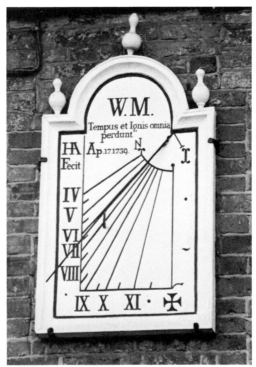

'Time and Fire consume all things'. This sundial in Stony Stratford commemorates some of the many fires in Stony. (NK)

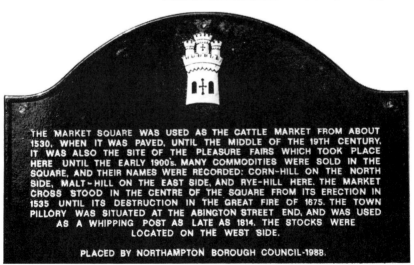

THE MARKET SQUARE WAS USED AS THE CATTLE MARKET FROM ABOUT 1530, WHEN IT WAS PAVED, UNTIL THE MIDDLE OF THE 19TH CENTURY. IT WAS ALSO THE SITE OF THE PLEASURE FAIRS WHICH TOOK PLACE HERE UNTIL THE EARLY 1900's. MANY COMMODITIES WERE SOLD IN THE SQUARE, AND THEIR NAMES WERE RECORDED: CORN-HILL ON THE NORTH SIDE, MALT-HILL ON THE EAST SIDE, AND RYE-HILL HERE. THE MARKET CROSS STOOD IN THE CENTRE OF THE SQUARE FROM ITS ERECTION IN 1535 UNTIL ITS DESTRUCTION IN THE GREAT FIRE OF 1675. THE TOWN PILLORY WAS SITUATED AT THE ABINGTON STREET END, AND WAS USED AS A WHIPPING POST AS LATE AS 1814. THE STOCKS WERE LOCATED ON THE WEST SIDE.

PLACED BY NORTHAMPTON BOROUGH COUNCIL-1988.

Historical Plaque in the Market Square, Northampton.

Chapter 18

Sermons in Stones

'And this our life, exempt from public haunt
Finds tongues in trees, books in the running brooks,
Sermons in stones, and good in everything'.
(Shakespeare: 'As You Like It')

Two celebrated buildings in Northamptonshire give us 'sermons in stones'. One is Castle Ashby, home of the Compton family since 1512, and the seat of the Earls of Northampton. All round the top of the house the parapet spells out, in Latin and in very large carved letters, words from Psalm 127:

Except the Lord build the house they labour but in vain that build it. Except the Lord keep the house the watchman waketh but in vain'.

This 'sermon in stone' was created in 1624.

Elsewhere at Castle Ashby a stone screen joins the ends of the two wings. Here too are Latin words carved in large letters – on one side: *'The Lord guard your coming in'* and on the other side: *'The Lord guard your going out'*.

These carvings were part of a 1730 alteration of the house.

The 19th century brought yet more 'sermons in stones', for in 1865 four large terraces were laid out, complete with stone fountains and shaped flower beds. Balustrades divide these and bear biblical quotations in carved letters: *'The grass withereth and the flower fadeth but the word of God endureth forever'. 'Consider the lilies of the field how they grow, they toil not neither do they spin and yet I say unto you that Solomon in all his glory was not arrayed like one of these'.*

Within the house there is a Chapel and in the Park near the

house stands the 14th century parish church of St. Mary Magdalene. On the skyline can be seen no less than seven churches. No wonder someone once said that Northamptonshire is renowned for its squires and spires!

Totally Triangular

There is no more astonishing example of 'sermons in stone' than the unique Triangular Lodge, three miles north of Kettering and one mile west of Rushton. It is indeed totally triangular. In plan it is an equilateral triangle. There are three storeys with three windows on each side of each floor. Each of the three sides has three gables, rising to three tapering pinnacles. On the roof is a three-sided chimney stack. A frieze running below the gables bears a continuous inscription carried on all three sides. Each side is thirty-three feet long, and each is inscribed with thirty-three letters.

The Triangular Lodge at Rushton is both an architectural curiosity and a theological statement. (JH)

The 'three-ness' is everywhere. The inscriptions are all in Latin. The first, over the entrance door, translated into English, says: 'There are three that bear witness'. The inscriptions on each of the three sides relate to the three Persons of the Trinity. Clearly, then, the whole building is meant to be a sermon on the Trinity. But more subtly it is also a sermon on the Mass. Some of the inscriptions are quotations from the Liturgy of the Mass. The structural arrangement of the central chimney stack is reminiscent of the Elevation of the Chalice at the Consecration.

It was Sir Thomas Tresham who designed the building and had it erected. Construction began in July 1594 and was completed in September 1597. The planning by Sir Thomas Tresham had occupied him many years, and for much of that time he was either in prison or under house arrest. He had become a Roman Catholic in 1580 and his repeated spells in prison were the price he paid for that fact. He decided to express his faith in architectural terms. His Triangular Lodge would be his 'sermon in stone'. Ostensibly the building would be a dwelling for the Warrener of the Rushton estate – a sort of gamekeeper responsible for the maintenance of the rabbit warrens which in those days were an important source of food.

The Triangular Lodge, then, was far from being a folly. It was well-designed and well-built. Its symbolism is there for all to see, an expression of loyalty to his faith made by Sir Thomas who had paid dearly for that faith.

'Old Scarlett'

Epitaphs and monuments can also be 'sermons in stone'. They record human mortality and are a reminder that death awaits us all! And when death comes, the Sexton has his part to play.

Perhaps no Sexton has a more remarkable story to tell than 'Old Scarlett' of Peterborough. He lived to the age of ninety-eight, dying on 2nd July 1591. So as Sexton he had buried two full generations of his fellow citizens. More remarkable still, it fell to his lot to bury two Queens, both of whom died in tragic circumstances. He performed his office for them both in Peterborough Cathedral.

The first was Catherine of Arragon, the divorced wife of Henry VIII. She died at Kimbolton Castle in 1536. The second was Mary, Queen of Scots. She had been executed in Fotheringay Castle in 1587.

Peterborough Abbey had been made a Cathedral in 1541. 'Old Scarlett', then in his prime at about forty-eight, was its Sexton and remained so for another fifty years. His long service is commemorated in the Cathedral twice over, both in words and in picture. Above his epitaph there is a portrait of him on the wall, showing him with a spade in his hand, and with a pickaxe by his side. And for good measure at his feet lies a human skull.

The epitaph below the portrait tells it all:

> 'You see old Scarlett's picture stand on hie;
> But at your feet here doth his body lye.
> His gravestone doth his age and death-time show,
> His office by heis tokens you may know.
> Second to none for strength and sturdy limn,
> A scare-babe voice, with visage grim;
> He had inter'd two queenes within this place,
> And this townes householders in his life's space
> Twice over; but at length his own time came,
> What he for others did, for him the same
> Was done. No doubt his soule doth live for aye
> In heaven, though his body clad in clay.'

Robert Chambers (who figures also in Chapter 14) wrote of 'Old Scarlett' in his 'Book of Days' last century:

> 'And what a lively effigy – short, stout, and self-complacent, perfectly satisfied, and perhaps even proud of his profession, and content to be exhibited with all his insignia about him. Two queens had passed through his hands into that bed which gives a lasting rest to queens and to peasants alike.'

(If 'Old Scarlett's' fame rests largely on the fact that he buried two tragic queens, the husband of Lady Mary Salter is honoured with a memorial dated 1631 in Iver Church in Buckinghamshire, because he was 'Full forty years a carver to two kings'.)

❖ ❖ ❖ ❖ ❖

Cockayne Hatley in Bedfordshire has two contrasting epitaphs. One is on the tombstone of six-year-old Margaret Henley, who was the inspiration for Wendy in J M Barrie's 'Peter Pan'. It reads:

> *'Nothing is here for tears*
> *Nothing to wail or beat the breast*
> *Nothing but what is well and fair.'*

The other, on the tombstone of little Margaret's father, is more sombre:

> *'So be passing,*
> *My task accomplished and the long day done,*
> *My wages taken and in my heart*
> *Some late lark singing.*
> *Let me be gathered to the quiet West,*
> *The sundown splendid and serene,*
> *Death.'*

❖ ❖ ❖ ❖ ❖

Shot by Banditti

Even more sombre is the memorial in the church at Wadenhoe in Northamptonshire:

'Sacred to the memory of Thomas Welch Hunt, late proprietor of the estate and manor of Wadenhoe, and of Caroline his wife . . . who were both cruelly shot by banditti near Paestrum in Italy on Friday the 3rd of December 1824. He died on the evening of the same day having nearly completed his twenty-eighth year. She

died on the morning of the following Sunday in the twenty-third year of her age after a union of scarcely ten months. Affording an impressive and mournful instance of the instability of human happiness.'

Having the Last Word
In 1756 Daniel Knight died in Luton. During his lifetime he had quarrelled with Samuel Marsom, a Luton Baptist. Knight had been forced to make a public apology. He carried his resentment for this right up to his death – and beyond! He arranged to have the last word even after death. So he is commemorated in Luton Parish Church, not with a 'sermon in stone' but with a riposte in brass. His brass reads:

> *'Here lyeth the body of Daniel Knight*
> *Who all my life time lived in spite.*
> *Base flatterers sought me to undoe*
> *And made me sign what was not true.*
> *Reader take care whene'er you venture*
> *To trust a canting false dissenter.*
> *Who died June 11th in the 61st*
> *Year of his age. 1756.'*

Chapter 19

Incomers

Over thousands of winters and summers
marking the passage of years
have been succeeding waves of Incomers
often bringing fears and tears.

They came at first across the sea,
Catevellauni, aiming to settle;
Those then here were forced to flee,
fearing foes full-armed with metal.

An Iron-Age civilisation of sorts
lasted hereabouts a while
till came a mightier foe in boats
that marched inland each Roman mile.

The Belgics then in their turn fled,
faced by Roman military might;
Victorious legions through the country spread,
for British and Belgics a fearful sight.

They built their roads across the land,
traversing Dunstable Downs,
with staging-posts at each twelfth mile –
those staging-posts would grow to towns.

One of them we would know as Fenny,
astride the famous Watling Street,
a market-place and home for many
where canal and Ouse would one day meet.

But long before then would the Romans depart,
leaving Britain and heading for home.
To stay in Britain they no longer had heart,
knowing the danger threatening Rome.

The Romano-British thus left in these regions
would not for long be left in peace.
Angles and Saxons would come in their legions
and this whole countryside would seize.

The Romano-British, faced with this test,
could not hope to hold the land.
Their only recourse was to flee further west,
leaving Angles and Saxons in full command.

Five more centuries would then come and go,
and Mid-Anglia would all-too slowly develop;
and the 11th century would bring a new foe,
and the Normans this country envelop.

Latin, Norman-French, and English would compete
as the tongue that all men should use,
till the pattern would one day be complete
and Shakespeare, Bacon, and Milton obey the Muse.

Move the story on – yet more winters and summers;
Watch our Mid-Anglia story unwind
as in there came yet more Incomers –
the 'Navvies', Incomers of a new kind.

They dug the canal and built the locks,
to give freight a way by water,
to connect inland parts with London docks
and make transport of goods much shorter.

The Railways next, with all this would mean,
to bring to these parts much employment,
transforming our whole country scene,
combining utility with enjoyment.

Next we must note a very special wave –
the Incomers to Bletchley Park,
who did so much our cause to save
in World War II when days were dark.

Northants, Bucks, and Beds and Herts,
A significant part of our nation,
With great towns and lovely rural parts.
We have cause for celebration.

Neighbouring counties each contribute their story
Of growth and much healthy development.
Each Shire has known its moments of glory,
And each also has known what danger has meant.

Chapter 20

The First Shall Be Last

This last chapter is all about FIRSTS. Each of our four shires can claim an impressive number of firsts. They range from the merely interesting, or even trivial, to the historically very important. Some are tragic, others sentimental. Some concern agriculture, and others the world of sport. Some are significant in the context of religion. And all of them reflect the enormous variety of human experience.

❖

Probably no one will want to dispute the claim of Saunders Duncombe of Battlesden, whose proud boast it was that he was the first man to introduce the Sedan Chair into England.

❖

There might be some rival claims to challenge Ashton's right to hold the World Conker Championship! It is held in that Northamptonshire town on the second Sunday every October.

❖

In the sporting world Aylesbury claims to have held the first Point to Point Steeplechase in England. It was run in 1835 from Waddeston Windmill to a field just below Aylesbury Church.

❖

In the 'Fruit & Veg.' category we have claims from Dorney in Buckinghamshire for the first-ever pineapple grown in England – in 1665. It was presented to King Charles II. And from Colnbrook, also in Buckinghamshire comes the claim for the first-ever Cox's Orange Pippin.

❖

In the world of print we have a wide variety of claims.

Thomas Payne of Brackley ran a bookshop in London. He was the first man ever to print and distribute a Catalogue. His first one, in February 1770 was so successful that he went on producing them annually until he retired.

Hedgerley in Buckinghamshire claims a whole raft of firsts. The Vicar there was the Reverend Theophilus Hill. But it was his son John who was the clever dick. He was the first recognised newspaper columnist, the first biologist to introduce Linnaeus' system of plant classifications; he wrote the first English book on honey, and was the first to advance in writing the notion that there is a link between tobacco and cancer.

❖

Who really started Sunday Schools? The statue to Robert Raikes on the Embankment in London says that he did – in 1780 in Gloucester. But in High Wycombe they know differently. There, Hannah Moore started a Sunday School in 1769 in her own house. Though a Methodist, she affiliated her Sunday School to the Parish Church, to which the children were taken after each session at her house. As well as receiving religious instruction the children were also taught to read and write. So Hannah was also a pioneer of primary education. A window in the Town Hall in High Wycombe commemorates her.

❖

Did England have the first Ombudsman? We owe this odd word to Sweden. In Scandinavia an Ombudsman was a Commissioner, charged with the duty of protecting the rights of individuals against infringement by the Government. Sweden has had once since 1809. Denmark appointed one in 1955, and Norway and New Zealand in 1962. Britain followed in 1967.

But it could be argued that Elizabeth I appointed an Ombudsman. He wasn't called that of course, but his job was to bring to the Queen petitions and complaints which needed her attention. He was Walter Haddon (1516–1571), of Lillingstone Dayrell in Buckinghamshire. Elizabeth called him her 'Master of Requests', but she made sure that his access to her was limited. One day, when he had at last managed to be admitted to her she said: 'Thy new boots stink'. To which Walter Haddon replied: 'Madam, it is not my boots which stink; it is the old stale petitions that have been so long in my bag unopened'.

❖

A very sad 'first' belongs to Northamptonshire. The first blood to be shed in the Civil War was as the result of an incident at Kilsby in August 1642. A small troop of Royalists rode into the village and shot dead a number of its inhabitants. This was two weeks before Charles I actually raised his Standard at Nottingham. Ironically, three years later, and only ten miles from Kilsby, there was fought at Naseby the battle which virtually ended the Civil War in Cromwell's favour.

❖

Communications provide other 'firsts'. Newport Pagnell's celebrated Tickford Iron Bridge was not the first in the country – that honour belongs to Telford. But Newport Pagnell's Iron Bridge is still in daily use – the oldest working cast-iron bridge in the world.

Tickford Bridge in Newport Pagnell, the oldest working cast-iron in the world. It opened on September 29th 1819. (NK)

Another notable bridge is Marlow's Suspension Bridge over the Thames. William Clark built it in 1834. It was so highly thought of that he was twice asked to repeat it – once for a new bridge at Hammersmith, and second for a new bridge in Hungary across the Danube, to join the twin cities of Buda and Pest.

❖

Milestones on roads go back a very long way. But Hertfordshire has the record for the first erection of regular milestones over a complete road. The road in question was from Barkway to Cambridge. Successive Masters of Trinity Hall, Cambridge, provided both the initiative and the finance, so between 1728 and 1732 the entire length of that road as 'mile-stoned'.

❖

In World War I forty Vickers Vimy bombers were built in Leighton Buzzard by Morgan and Co., a firm which formerly built carriages and early motor cars. The fuselages of the planes, with wings removed, were towed through the street of Leighton Buzzard to Scotts Field on the edge of town. There, the wings were replaced and pilots from the Royal Flying Corp flew them off.

❖

War Memorials are uncountable. There is one which commemorates, not the soldiers who fell in battle, but a horse. It is at Latimer in Buckinghamshire. On Latimer Village Green an Obelisk was erected in memory of those who fell in the Boer War. Alongside that Obelisk is another memorial. Its plaque records that buried on that spot is: 'The horse ridden by General de Villebois Mareuil at the Battle of Boshof, South Africa, in which the General was killed and his horse wounded'. A second inscription adds: 'Villebois brought to England by Major General Lord Chesham KCB in 1900'.

❖

In a class on its own is the 'first' which relates to Bletchley Park. The world now knows a great deal of what went on there during World War II, and how the efforts of some 1,200 men and women employed there went a very long way to winning the war for the Allies. Dwight Eisenhower himself wrote: 'It has saved thousands of British and American lives and in no small way contributed to the speed with which the enemy was routed and eventually forced to surrender'.

In essence it was a gigantic code-breaking operation in which those at Bletchley Park, using the Germans' own Enigma machine and all its variants, were able to read all the signals sent by German High Command to all its units of land, sea and air forces. It has aptly been described as 'Britain's Best Kept Secret'. That it remained totally secret is astounding, given the huge number of people employed.

One of that host has written the following, anonymously:

BLETCHLEY PARK

> *To think that I should ever see*
> *a sight so curious as BP,*
> *a place called up at war's behest*
> *and peopled with the queerly-dressed.*
> *Yet what they did they could not say*
> *nor ever shall till Judgment Day.*
>
> *For 6 long years have we been there*
> *subject to local scorn and stare.*
> *We came by transport and by train,*
> *the dull, the brilliantly insane.*
> *What were we for? Where shall be be*
> *When God at last redunds BP?*
>
> *The Air Force types who never fly,*
> *Soldiers who never do or die,*
> *Land-lubber Sailors, beards complete,*
> *Long-haired civilians, slim, effete.*
> *Why they were they they never knew*
> *And what they told you wasn't true.*

If I should die, think this of me
I served my country at BP.
And should my son ask :'What did you
in the Atomic World War do?'
God only knows – and He won't tell,
for after all BP was Hell!

Bletchley Park, 'the best kept secret of World War II'. (JH)

❖

If the whole astonishing story of Bletchley Park constitutes a 'first', within that story there is an inner 'first'. For at Bletchley Park there was assembled and used the world's first computer.

In the summer of 1943 a machine called 'Colossus' was introduced into Bletchley Park. It was a remarkable breakthrough. Its photo-electric punched-tape reader was capable of processing 5,000 characters per second. Within twelve months other 'Colossi' were developed to read 25,000 characters per second. The concept had first been explored by the eccentric mathematician Alan Turing. Developing his work Professor Max Newman and T H Flowers created 'Colossus'.

They had succeeded in making the first practical application of electronic decision-making circuitry, and in so doing they created the fore-runner of post-war digital computers.

Bletchley Park

In the 55 acres of Bletchley Park the German 'Enigma' machine was mastered, and the world's first Computer was set up.

'Colossus' remained a closely guarded secret until it was declassified in 1975, though the technical achievements it represented found their way into a commercial environment soon after the War. The pioneer work of Turing, Newman, and

Flowers marked a great watershed, and Bletchley Park can rightly claim to be the birthplace of today's modern computer industry.

❖ ❖ ❖ ❖ ❖

This last chapter of 'firsts' is far from complete. Other firsts remain to be honoured. None of those mentioned here, and none of those not included, can compare with the 'first' which belongs to Hertfordshire, and was the subject of Chapter 11. It dates back over 1600 years – the story of Alban, England's first Christian Martyr.

INDEX

A

Abbots Langley, 39
Abthorpe, 41
Akeman Street, 103
Alban, Saint, 79, 130
Alfred the Great, 23
Amersham, 84
Amwellbury, 43
Amphibalus, 79
Anne, Queen, 10
Ashby St. Ledger, 73
Ashendon, 88
Ashwell, 43
Aspley Guise, 87
Aston Clinton, 61
Atterbury, Francis, 10
Aylesbury, 7, 30, 91, 108, 123

B

Banastre, Robert, 40
Barn Preachers, 100
Bassetbury, 66
Battlesden, 123
Beaconsfield, 15
Bede, 82
Bedford, 7, 68
Belch, Sir Toby, 85
Bells, 59, 85
Berkhamstead, 28, 49
Bicester, 103
Bishopstone, 66
Black Death, 62, 109
Bletchley, 23, 31, 92
Bletchley Park, 126
Boughton, 4
Bradbrook, William, 27, 101
Brickhills, 2
Brixworth, 55

Brocas, Sir Pexall, 2
Buckingham, 57, 90
Bulstrode, 3
Burgwash, Bishop, 5

C

Cadman, Robert, 56
Cambridge, 50
Canals, 36, 90, 103
Carrington, Lord, 66
Cassiobury, 41
Castle Ashby, 9, 10, 14
Catesby, Robert, 73
Catherall, George, 4
Catherine of Aragon, 117
Chalgrave, 7, 16
Chandler family, 59
Chambers, Robert, 94, 117
Charles I, 6, 75
Charles II, 40, 42, 73, 111
Churchill, Charles, 20
Churchill, Winston, 42
Chicksands, 38
Chiltern Hundreds, 97
Cholera, 111
Civil War, 6, 41, 125
Claydon, 28
Cockayne Hatley, 118
Colnbrook, 88, 123
Colossus, 128
Compton, Henry, 9
Computer, first, 128
Conker Championship, 123
Constantine, Emperor, 80
Cowper, William, 44, 84
Cromwell, Oliver, 76, 98
Cublington, 28

D

Danes, Danelaw, 23
Dashwood, Sir Francis, 69, 95
Denham, 94
Digby, Sir Everard, 73, 95
Dodd, William, 16
Domesday, 24
Dorchester Abbey, 26
Drayton Parslow, 59
Dunstable, 4, 105, 106

E

Eddlesborough, 4
Eleanor Crosses, 105
Elizabeth I, 76, 124
Enigma Machine, 127
Epidemics, 31

F

Farnham Royal, 84
Fawkes, Guy, 74
Fenny Stratford, 27, 33, 110
Ferrars, Lady Catherine, 2
Fingest, 5
Fires, 109
Foscote, 103
Fosse Way, 103
Fotheringay Castle, 117
Fulmer, 43

G

Gayhurst, 73, 95
Geoffrey, Bishop, 30
Gerards Cross, 3
Glorious Revolution, 4
Gould, John, 15
Great Horwood, 112
Great Linford, 60
Great Munden, 87
Grey family, 30
Gribble, 'General', 67
Guilds, 32
Gunpowder Plot, 73

H

Haggy, Mother, 42
Hanmer 'Tally! Ho', 14
Hampden, John, 5
Hanslope, 28, 56, 57, 112
Hastings, Battle of, 28
Harold, King, 28
Hatfield House, 43
Hell Fire Club, 69
Hockliffe, 16
Hoddeston, 77
High Wycombe, 124
Hogarth, William, 70
Howard, John, 7
Holtspur, 16
Hundreds, 23
Huntingdon, 51

I

Icknield Way, 102
Ivinghoe Aston, 2
Ivinghoe Beacon, 4, 102

J

James, Jesse, 22
James I, 30, 40
James II, 3, 10, 73
Jefferys, Judge, 3

K

Kettering, 115
Kimbolton Castle, 117
Knight, Daniel, 119

L

Lace-making, 35
Lanfranc, Archbishop, 26
Leighton Buzzard, 36, 92, 99, 126
Levellers, 64
Lillingstone Dayrell, 95, 124
Lincoln, 5, 33, 61, 79
Linslade, 28, 61

Little Brickhill, 2
Little Horwood, 88
Liverpool, 49
London, 9
Long Crendon, 66
Loudwater, 66
Luton, 67, 110, 119

M
Machine Breakers, 64
Mad Monks, 20, 69
Magiovinium, 28, 29, 79
'Magnificent Seven', 10
Markyate, 2
Marlow, 65, 126
Marsh Green, 66
Marsom, Samuel, 119
Mason, John, 18
Marston Moretaine, 61
Mary I, 76
Medmenham, 20, 69
Mercia, 23, 28, 80
Milton Keynes, 10
Milestones, 126
Minsden, 38
Missendon, 71
Moore, Hanna, 124

N
Nash, 65
Newell, Joseph, 12
Newton, 64
Newton, John, 44
Newport Pagnell, 30, 125
Normans, 24
Northampton, 4, 62, 91, 111
Norwich, 63

O
Offa, King, 80
Olney, 44, 56, 87
Ombudsman, 124
Orange, William of, 78

Orchards Side, Olney, 52
Oundle, 64
Ouzel R, 27
Oxford, 30

P
Parker, 58
Passenahm, 39
Peasants' Revolt, 62
Penn, 4
Peterborough, 63, 116
Pirton, 43
Pineapple, first, 123
Pitstone, 102
Plague, 33, 109
Poll Tax, 62
Pouch, 'Captain', 64
Prison Reform, 8
Puddingstone, 86

Q
Queen Anne's Bounty, 34

R
Railways, 36, 90
Raikes, Robert, 124
Raunds, 67
Reynolds, John, 64
Richard II, 62
Ridgeway, 102
Risborough, 28
Rockingham Forest, 86
Rombold, 77
Russell, William, 77
Rye House Plot, 73

S
Sarratt, 43
Saxons, 25
St. Albans, 41, 79, 103 110
Scandinavia, 124
Scarlett, Old, 116
Schools, 35

Sheriffs, 21
Shires, 21
Shrimpton, Jack, 4
Simpson, 14, 28
Slash, 'Captain', 4
Slave Trade, 46
Slough, 66
Soulbury, 86
Steeplejacks, 56
Stamp Duty, 100
Stevenage, 1
Stoke Hammond, 15
Stony Stratford, 23, 30, 85, 103, 111
Stowe, 88, 90
Sundial, Stony Stratford, 112
Swing, 'Captain', 65

T
Thames, 126
Thrapston, 64
Thornborough, 12
Thornton, 13
Tickford Bridge, 125
Trayli, Sir Walter, 96
Tresham, 116
Trigg, Henry, 1
Tring, 4, 39
Triangular Lodge, 115
Tornado, 60
Towcester, 79
Turnpikes, 105
Tyburn, 4, 16
Tyringham, 74
Tyler, Wat, 63

U
Unwin, Mary, 50
Unwin, Morley, 50

V
Vale of Aylesbury, 24
Verulamium, 79
Villiers, 30

W
Waddeston, 28, 123
Water Eaton, 28
Water Stratford, 18
Wallingford, 24
Wansford, 1
Ware, 85
Wavendon, 65
Wedenhoe, 118
West Wycombe, 20, 69, 87
Wessex, 23
Westminster Abbey, 11, 24
Weston Underwood, 53
Whaddon, 31
Whitehead, Paul, 95
Wilberforce, William, 53
William, of Orange, 4, 10, 78
William, the Conqueror, 24
Willis, Browne, 13, 33, 58
Willis, Thomas, 31
Winchendon, 98
Wilkes, John, 20, 70
Wolverton, 28
Woodford, 95

Y
Yardley Chase, 84

Books Published by THE BOOK CASTLE

JOURNEYS INTO HERTFORDSHIRE: Anthony Mackay.
Foreword by The Marquess of Salisbury, Hatfield House. Nearly 200 superbly detailed ink drawings depict the towns, buildings and landscape of this still predominantly rural county.

JOURNEYS INTO BEDFORDSHIRE: Anthony Mackay.
Foreword by The Marquess of Tavistock, Woburn Abbey. A lavish book of over 150 evocative ink drawings.

NORTH CHILTERNS CAMERA, 1863–1954: From the Thurston Collection in Luton Museum: edited by Stephen Bunker.
Rural landscapes, town views, studio pictures and unique royal portraits by the area's leading early photographer.

LEAFING THROUGH LITERATURE: Writers' Lives in Hertfordshire and Bedfordshire: David Carroll.
Illustrated short biographies of many famous authors and their connections with these counties.

THROUGH VISITORS' EYES: A Bedfordshire Anthology:
edited by Simon Houfe.
Impressions of the county by famous visitors over the last four centuries, thematically arranged and illustrated with line drawings.

THE HILL OF THE MARTYR: An Architectural History of St. Albans Abbey: Eileen Roberts.
Scholarly and readable chronological narrative history of Hertfordshire and Bedfordshire's famous cathedral. Fully illustrated with photographs and plans.

LOCAL WALKS: South Bedfordshire and North Chilterns:
Vaughan Basham. Twenty-seven thematic circular walks.

LOCAL WALKS: North and Mid-Bedfordshire:
Vaughan Basham. Twenty-five thematic circular walks.

CHILTERN WALKS: Hertfordshire, Bedfordshire and North Buckinghamshire: Nick Moon.
Part of the trilogy of circular walks, in association with the Chiltern Society. Each volume contains thirty circular walks.

CHILTERN WALKS: Buckinghamshire: Nick Moon.

CHILTERN WALKS: Oxfordshire and West Buckinghamshire:
Nick Moon.

OXFORDSHIRE WALKS: Oxford, the Cotswolds and the Cherwell Valley: Nick Moon.
One of two volumes planned to complement Chiltern Walks: Oxfordshire and complete coverage of the county, in association with the Oxford Fieldpaths Society.

LEGACIES: Tales and Legends of Luton and the North Chilterns:
Vic Lea. Twenty-five mysteries and stories based on fact, including
Luton Town Football Club. Many photographs.

ECHOES: Tales And Legends of Bedfordshire and Hertfordshire
Vic Lea. Thirty, compulsively retold historical incidents.

MURDERS and MYSTERIES, PEOPLE and PLOTS:
A Buckinghamshire, Bedfordshire and Northamptonshire
Miscellany: John Houghton. This fascinating book of true tales
roams around three counties and covers three centuries.

BEDFORDSHIRE'S YESTERYEARS: The Family, Childhood and
Schooldays: Brenda Fraser-Newstead.
Unusual early 20th century reminiscences, with private photographs.
Three further themed collections planned.

WHIPSNADE WILD ANIMAL PARK: 'MY AFRICA': Lucy Pendar.
Foreword by Andrew Forbes. Introduction by Gerald Durrell. Inside
story of sixty years of the Park's animals and people – full of
anecdotes, photographs and drawings.

FARM OF MY CHILDHOOD, 1925–1947: Mary Roberts.
An almost vanished lifestyle on a remote farm near Flitwick.

A LASTING IMPRESSION: Michael Dundrow. An East End boy's
wartime experiences as an evacuee on a Chilterns farm at Totternhoe.

EVA'S STORY: Chesham Since the Turn of the Century: Eva Rance
The ever-changing twentieth-century, especially the early years at her
parents' general stores, Tebby's, in the High Street.

DUNSTABLE DECADE: THE EIGHTIES: – A Collection of
Photographs: Pat Lovering.
A souvenir book of nearly 300 pictures of people and events in the 1980s.

DUNSTABLE IN DETAIL: Nigel Benson.
A hundred of the town's buildings and features, plus town trail map.

OLD DUNSTABLE: Bill Twaddle.
A new edition of this collection of early photographs.

BOURNE AND BRED: A Dunstable Boyhood Between the Wars:
Colin Bourne.
An elegantly written, well-illustrated book capturing the spirit of the
town over fifty years ago.

ROYAL HOUGHTON: Pat Lovering.
Illustrated history of Houghton Regis from the earliest times to the
present.

COUNTRY AIR: SUMMER and AUTUMN: Ron Wilson.
The Radio Northampton presenter looks month by month at the
countryside's wildlife, customs and lore.

COUNTRY AIR: WINTER and SPRING: Ron Wilson.
This companion volume completes the year in the countryside.

THE CHANGING FACE OF LUTON: An Illustrated History:
Stephen Bunker, Robin Holgate and Marian Nichols.
Luton's development from earliest times to the present busy industrial town. Illustrated in colour and monochrome. The three authors from Luton Museum are all experts in local history, archaeology, crafts and social history.

THE MEN WHO WORE STRAW HELMETS: Policing Luton, 1840–1974: Tom Madigan.
Meticulously chronicled history; dozens of rare photographs; author served Luton Police for nearly fifty years. '

BETWEEN THE HILLS: The Story of Lilley, a Chiltern Village:
Roy Pinnock.
A priceless piece of our heritage – the rural beauty remains but the customs and way of life described here have largely disappeared.

THE TALL HITCHIN SERGEANT: A Victorian Crime Novel based on fact: Edgar Newman.
Mixes real police officers and authentic background with an exciting storyline.

Specially for Children

ADVENTURE ON THE KNOLLS: A Story of Iron Age Britain:
Michael Dundrow.
Excitement on Totternhoe Knolls as ten-year-old John finds himself back in those dangerous times, confronting Julius Caesar and his army.

THE RAVENS: One Boy Against the Might of Rome:
James Dyer.
On the Barton Hills and in the south-each of England as the men of the great fort of Ravensburgh (near Hexton) confront the invaders.

Further titles are in preparation.
All the above are available via any bookshop, or from the publisher and bookseller

THE BOOK CASTLE
12 Church Street, Dunstable, Bedfordshire, LU5 4RU
Tel: (0582) 605670